No Stone Unturned

The Remapping of Broken Ideals

ALEX VASQUEZ

© 2022 by Alex Vasquez

All rights reserved. No part of this book may be reproduced or transmitted in any form or by any means, electronic or mechanical, including photocopying, recording, or by any information storage and retrieval system, except in the case of brief quotations embodied in critical articles and reviews, without prior written permission of the publisher.

Although the author and publisher have made every effort to ensure the accuracy and completeness of information contained in this book, we assume no responsibility for errors, inaccuracies, omissions, or any inconsistency herein.

Printed in the United States of America.

ISBN: 978-1-7340212-3-3

CONTENTS

FORWORD 5

ACKNOWLEDGMENTS 7

INTRODUCTION 13

CHAPTER 1 17
LOVE CONQUERS ALL *(Except when you add stuff like alcohol, drugs, cheating, abuse, or a traumatic childhood)*

CHAPTER 2 31
FAMILY & MARRIAGE SHOULD BE LIFE GOALS *(Except if you had poor examples growing up, then just getting your shit together should be the goal)*

CHAPTER 3 55
TIME HEALS EVERYTHING *(Except if you don't work on the issues, or live in denial and distractions)*

CHAPTER 4 63
IT'S BEST TO WAIT TO HAVE SEX UNTIL YOU'RE MARRIED *(Except for the people who don't wait)*

CHAPTER 5 79
BLOOD IS THICKER THAN WATER *(Except when your rich father dies)*

CHAPTER 6 89
HAVING COMPASSION MAKES YOU A GOOD PERSON *(Except when you have an agenda)*

CHAPTER 7 101
YOU DESERVE RESPECT *(Except when you don't care what anyone thinks)*

CHAPTER 8 115
THE WORLD OWES YOU SOMETHING *(Except, it really doesn't)*

CHAPTER 9 125
FULFILLMENT LIES IN ACCOMPLISHMENT *(Except, the perfect action has no result)*

CHAPTER 10 133
YOU CAN ONLY DIE ONCE *(Except when you understand you really must die each day)*

CHAPTER 11 147
A LETTER. DEAR TREVOR. IT IZ WHAT IT IZ *(Conclusion)*

FORWORD

I was once told that in order for things to move forward I had to be set free. To be enabled to fly. I was also told that someone had to get out of my way and that they could not give me what I needed in life.

The irony of these statements, by both of these people, was that the first person could at times fly much higher than me. Countless moments I observed with joy, just how high and marveled at their natural abilities. Unfortunately, what I could see so clearly was often not so clear to them.

The second person also could never fully grasp their strengths within and did not realize that I had already been given what I wanted. That it was them, who seemed to be getting in their own way.

Although this book stems from many rivers, these two people and specific statements, are what lit the fire inside me. In doing so changed my mind and heart for forever. Love needs no defense and truth always provides freedom. Just because we can't understand it, doesn't make it false. Only when you leave no stone unturned in your heart will you find the peace you deserve. To those two people, I love you and will keep you close to my heart for eternity.

ACKNOWLEDGMENTS

To my mother. Thank you for keeping me on the path.
My guardian.

To my father. Free at last.
My rebel.

To Amy. I'll see you again, in this life or the next. Don't forget.
My greatest teacher.

To my team @ Rhino. I'm able to do this because of what you do for me.
Forever grateful.

To Jayla. Thank you for giving me such a gift, even if only for a short moment in time.
My mirror.

THANK YOU

ACKNOWLEDGMENTS | 9

THANK YOU

THANK YOU

"Here is my book on forgiving
The pages are well worn
Here are the places I struggle
Here are the places I passed through with ease
Here is my book of forgiving
Some of its pages are tear-stained and torn
Some are decorated with joy and laughter
Some of its pages are written with hope
Some are etched with despair
This is my book of forgiving
This book is full of stories and secrets
It tells you how I finally broke free from being defined by injury
And chose to become a creator again
Offering forgiveness
Accepting that I am forgiven
Creating a world of peace"

—DESMOND TUTU

INTRODUCTION

Just start. You know it's time, and the journey begins with the first step or word. Venturing from the real estate world, where I developed years and years of foundation and mastery, to now transitioning about writing topics, that at face value, seem to have little to no connection. However, the correlation between self-help, psychology, sexism, and faith, seeming initially like a melting pot of social discord, once deeply analyzed, have a very profound and synchronistic harmony. But, before we dive into whatever the hell that means, let's first dissect the title, the origin of this book and why you are here.

Growing up, we develop a map of life and its ideals. As we mature, gradually it fills with the most basic rules, from how to tie one's shoes to more extreme and very complex beliefs and assumptions, such as one's faith or religion.

However, through the years, the "truth" of what we have come to believe, versus the harsh reality of what the world prescribes, often, and most likely will, completely eradicate the map we have been using. The same map that at one time helped guide us.

Depending on the severity of the impact and meaning of that shaken ideal, for many, losing what we thought we knew can come as a shock of denial or detachment. For others, the broken ideal can be exactly what they need to level up for continued growth. But there are also many people for whom, when life's storm rips out a part of them that is so innate and familiar, their entire world collapses. This can leave one feeling as if a part of themselves has been amputated.

Like being a foreigner in a new place, without a map to guide you, each step can feel so overwhelming, many don't dare to move at all. This petrified state can result in our lives becoming stagnant, and in feeling hyper anxious, bitter, resentful, lost, or even malevolent.

If your map has been shattered and you are like a ship at sea that has lost its north star, this book is for you.

So, what is to be done when the "truths" that we have come to know, understand, define ourselves as or even worship, come crashing down? Many people think rebuilding is a good start. But like a worker ant, if you continue to build the same way, in the same area and expect different results, you'll be bound for more disappointment. For these types, maybe the trauma was not big enough, and the same lesson, ten times over, will need to be dispensed for it to register.

For those that have been forever changed, forever moved, forever impacted, but just don't know why or what's next, I hope that the pages throughout this book can be your guide. I cannot guarantee that my map and understanding will be a perfect fit for you. But I can say that my reasoning comes from the sole purpose of throwing out enough lifelines and ideas to help you find yourself again. Help you work with the building of your new ideals. Help you question the status quo of a society and culture that thinks "Happily ever after" is the decree, when in fact it's more of the exception than the rule. And why, like the phoenix, we must burn and die each day, to only rise again, stronger. As someone who has been to hell and back on more than one occasion, I would like to think that every time the devil knows I'm coming to see him, he shudders at the thought, because he knows how hard this man has fought and will fight, to climb out of the deepest and darkest pits.

This is why I wrote this book. I was desperate and I had lost my ability to move PRODUCTIVELY due to my incapacity to access anything more than I already knew. I had taken it to the end, and in doing so, had found out just how much I did not know, but more important, what I needed to learn.

If your map has failed you, that's okay. It just means it's time to reroute it. But be warned, configuring a new map will be a monumental task. It will require going backwards as much as forwards and will necessitate the will to question age-old beliefs, cultural norms, stigmas, and concepts. Knowing this, many just stay where they are because the pain of this journey is too daunting to scale in their minds.

Indeed, this is a hero's journey. Only until we have been stripped of everything, can we accept that what we need has yet to be mapped out. It's through this process where truth can be found and through truth, you can hope to find your peace.

Alex

CHAPTER 1

LOVE CONQUERS ALL
*(Except when you add stuff like alcohol, drugs,
cheating, abuse, or a traumatic childhood)*

"The love we give away, is the only love we keep."
—ELBERT HUBBARD

Once upon a time there lived a fair maiden, possessing all the attributes any man could seek. Kind beyond measure, intelligent, and leading her class in every way possible. Athletic, and holding records in her chosen sport, artistic in music and art and with a voice so sweet, the gods could only smile when they heard her song. Traditional, enjoying first to tend to the daily chores and cooking the family meal. And no one could be more enthusiastic about one day starting a family of her own. Indeed, an exemplary mother and wife she could one day be. Her beauty is beyond what words can describe. Tall, lithe, and curvy, with flowing golden hair, piercing blue or green eyes (depending on what she wore and the light in the sky). Seeing this wonder enlightens us as to why men throughout the ages have sacrificed everything to win the favor of such a woman.

The man in this story, also being deemed worthy of such a companion through his attributes, is described in a hero's manner. Strong enough to conquer any task at hand, but sensitive enough to find compassion and understanding for all. Brave and protecting, always putting others first and ensuring that the end results lead to the whole being better and not just for his personal gain. Wise, cultured, and well-traveled, letting his actions lead the way and never mandating any advice unless first asked for insight and help. Humble and gracious in victory or defeat and wanting always, everyone to win, more than wanting to be right. With a warrior's spirit and a resolve that could not be shaken, this man's empire would be hard pressed to ever be upset with such a fair maiden by his side. The pair had no other place to go, but to the pinnacle of what two dynamic people like this could achieve.

The map has been set, the foundation of a specific way of life, or ideals. For most of us, this is deeply attributed with the desire to "check the boxes" of this fairytale or similar stories. Being more interested in what we think it "should be" versus the harsh reality of what it truly is. Ideals are the cornerstones in our lives and can guide us to salvation, but as you evolve, or your situation changes, in many instances in ways for which you are not prepared, holding on to the same ideals can cause you to be trapped in an unyielding pattern and prevent you from the growth necessary to raise you out of chaos.

This is where I found myself. This is the first of ten ideals that had failed me. And as hard as I had worked to achieve them and an understanding of what love "should be", I would have to work twice as hard to remap my course. My survival and sanity truly depended on it, or I knew I would be caught in an unforgiving cycle, that if I did not take it seriously, could bury me forever.

Back to the introductory fairytale. For me, being the best and almost Spartan like in discipline, enabled a machine type pace. Sacrificing the moment for something greater in the future, for not only myself, but for my loved ones. Taking notes and guidance from the greatest men in history, my aim for achievement and accomplishment was an almost maniac type of mission. The ideal seemed to have all the ingredients to justify years of my eighty-hour work weeks and little to no time for anything or anyone. My maiden, honoring the ideal in her best way, ventured down her own path as well. With the vision to complete her education and line up with my company's eventual success, that would surely enable a family, the freedom to stay at home and frequent vacations around the world. The ideal had held but as it edged closer to what appeared to be "Happily ever after" the wheels started falling off and when you're moving at such a pace, there are bound to be causalities.

When I first thought of what an ideal was constructed of, in this case, romantic love, I truly thought that through everything, no matter how bad it got, that love would prevail. Kind of like a one size fits all type situation, velcro on shoes, or ordering something on Amazon. Click and you're done. I'm far from naïve, so please don't get me wrong when I say that it's obvious that some things can get so bad that even for the best of us, they are hard to overcome. All relationships take a ton of work and dedication, but to me, that came with the territory and wasn't a factor that concerned me. Of course, that was at the beginning. But as the company solidified, school for her finished and the path cleared from what was once a factory line type approach, the ideal of what got me through the previous chapter, showed me nothing in regards on how to deal with love, specifically when trust on both sides had been damaged.

As humans, we are predisposed in many ways, and ironically, our default is to avoid pain more than to seek pleasure. You have probably heard that when given the option, people would rather not find money on the street than lose the same amount. So, basically, losing five dollars is worse than finding it! Understanding this simple, yet intuitive emotional prerequisite, gives you a better idea of why it is so hard for us to change ideals, especially if, for the most part, they are "working". The term, "don't rock the boat" or "if it's not broken, don't fix it" gives a feeble cover, especially when real change is needed to salvage what's left. But the work that is vital to change, often burdens our attention to core ideals for which we have no other alternative. Seemingly, making it easier to ignore or "accept" them, versus putting in the work, knowing that in the process, the house could come falling down. You'd think it logical to take that chance and that love would help get you through it. But in my case, you'd be wrong.

GETTING UNSTUCK

So why do we stay stuck in relationships that are clearly not functioning properly or have failed to evolve to higher plains? I can say that from my personal experience, there is not a clear-cut answer. The combination of what molded our personalities to how we perceive life and our core values, coupled with the onslaught of daily life, is a matrix of innumerable amalgamations. So much so, that based on the history of human nature, it's quite clear that we are yet to provide an answer.

I believe that for most of us, the examples we are provided on which to base our ideals are too generic to hold profound insight into life after the honeymoon. Happily ever after always sounds nice, however,

Disney conveniently skipped the entire chapters to what happens in the post phases of a relationship. Only through trial and error can we adapt and hopefully grow, yet growth in uncharted territory can have severe risks and pitfalls. Learning, as you go in relationships, can be a double-edged sword, where the peaks can be remarkable, but the valleys may be insurmountable. Love alone, although a good compass, does not always provide you with the rationale of a major block between two people. So, what defines a major block? Again, another million-dollar question and entirely objective for the individual. Nonetheless, I think there are universal truths that each person holds dear. In fact, there may be several of these "truths" we undervalue or excuse in the "name of love", sacrificing who we are for an ideal that initially had no explicit instructions. Vis-à-vis, "Love conquering all". To think we can supplement our inner truths for another, in hopes that what has been sacrificed will somehow balance the relationship, is a recipe for disaster. Love has no judgment and should not be held hostage. Sadly, love makes a hell of an argument and, in contrast, the fear of losing your relationship repeatedly trumps one's desire to challenge one's fears. Often, it is in the places we least want to look or work on where the most profound clarity and growth happens. Making it a good argument on why settling for less than desirable relationships tends to be the rule, rather than the exception. It takes great courage to be confident and to be ok with what you believe and to stand by it. But it takes even greater strength to face the unknown of the consequences those beliefs will have, often losing the one you love and having to proceed alone.

This is exactly where I found myself. Alone. My map and assumptions had dissolved and no relief for the pain and confusion was in sight. Mentally and emotionally, I was drained beyond measure and physically suffering from symptoms of a chronic and endless battle to hold a relationship together. The truth of my situation that ensued revealed not only the tangible reality of the loss, but the subconscious fears that I had been harboring.

And in this situation is where the defining choices for most of us begin. Where the map has ended and where habits can be broken or reengaged. When you are faced with what appears to be a negative outcome (in this case a botched relationship) the first thoughts are typically to blame, avoid, deny, or replace. And for good reason. For any extended relationship (five years +) there is far too much history and information to be able to sift through and come up with a specific "why". Not to mention your post relationship, and any family issues that accompanied it. Relationships don't generally just stop in one day, but as time passes, it's the issues that are not addressed, that tend to buildup resentment and become the catalyst for the "last straw". Making the end of the relationship the most recent and most clear, however not necessarily the most impactful in regard to pinpointing where to find the prime examples of what could have been the crux of the breakdown. But at this crucial time is where the work comes in and where most run right back into the same patterns. In our minds, what we knew (previously had mapped out) is easy to jump back into. However, when faced with the unknown, and the demons that rest there, it may just be to overwhelming. The painful actions of your partner in a relationship can open the door, but it's rare that they are the sole cause of the failures and your pain.

So, what to do? The simple answer—jump in the pain. Don't blame anyone, it's better to reflect. Don't avoid the pain, it will continue to grow and always be there to greet you. Don't deny the pain.

Accepting that it happened is the first step to knowing what part of it was your doing. Don't replace the pain. Trying to do so is like filling a bottomless well. Nothing outside of you can ever make it right, no matter how you try.

He cheated; she was an alcoholic; he worked too much; she was jealous; he didn't like my family… Most of us have heard or experienced at least one of these in a relationship, if not several. And although they all can be grounds for the demise of a relationship, it's rare we question the "why's" behind the blame. Doing so would require work. A lot of work. And on top of that, you risk finding out things about yourself or partner that may not be reparable or are so deeply rooted that once discovered, the chances of rekindling become bleak. The issues of the moment need to be acknowledged and tackled with vigilance. Failure to do so will only delay the inevitable. However, many of us don't understand that lifetimes can be lost in the blame game, creating a toxic cycle that provides a slow death within. The faster we reflect, the sooner we can decide if we want to fix our issues. If we fix our issues and the problems in the relationship persist, then we can have a clearer conscience about the entire situation.

Assuming you still have gas in the tank and want to salvage and mend your relationship, one of the first steps is to **create a plan.** Procrastination is the deathblow of anything in life and in a relationship that is bruised and battered, each day that passes without a clear agenda, is one argument closer to total breakdown. The person you love needs to be a part of your life goals, and this requires a consistent, dedicated, and regimented approach. Examples, such as setting certain days and times each week to talk about core disputes and what compromises need to take place, are a proactive first step. There also need to be days that are just for you both to relax and feel safe, whether that is a quiet day at the house relaxing and watching your favorite movies or shows, or a day excursion to a new experience you both have been wanting to explore. Finding balance through the tough emotional work and then being able to have some "together time" to help heal will be necessary if you are to make it work.

For each person and for each relationship, "the plan" will be unique. But before a strategy starts, there's a bigger question to consider. Is there even a desire and commitment to carry it out? There is nothing worse than being in a relationship where the mindset of one, or both, is waiting for the other person to change. Or, just as bad, trying to change the other person. The premise of your relationship needs to be based on core understandings that you choose to accept about one another. Examples such as your partner being extroverted and you being more private, you having a loving family, while your partner has struggles with their family dynamic, or having different expressions regarding your "love language" are all-encompassing "defaults" that need to be embodied. You can't change a person's upbringing, especially if they have been raised by abusive or alcoholic parents or have grown up in a different culture. You can't change these things, so it's better to truly understand what that means prior to making up your game plan and how that will affect the approach.

But again, this rarely is taught and as kind and optimistic as you want to feel about love, very specific tools and insights need to be acknowledged as you venture into conquering it. Forcing a square peg into a round hole won't work and yet we are taught to believe that love is the one size fits all or the WD40, that will help slide things neatly into place. Love is messy, love is raw, love is a million shades of grey and never black and white. The quicker we realize this, the more we can accept the polarizing reality of situations that occur. The times when your resolve is truly tested can be the times that you learn the crucial life lessons of love.

The next step is to **learn how to argue.** Most of us think that remembering anniversaries, birthdays, setting "alone time" or date night, are on the top of the priority list when it comes to sustaining a relationship. Although not to be ignored, I came to realize that what was more important when re-designing my map, was learning how to argue. It's simple really, when times are good, who doesn't enjoy their anniversary dinner, or vacation to a dream destination? It's nothing really hard to prepare for when it's all said and done. But when situations become difficult, we are rarely trained for how to handle them. When we argue, many people resort to old defenses, rational and or justifications and nothing truly gets solved. The reason you typically get into a fight is because you are not seeing eye to eye and are stuck. So, the last thing you want to do is the same thing you have always done. Here are some examples of reactions and how they can be defined:

> THE RUNNER—This kind of personality does not like confrontations or being called out and would rather avoid conflict than deal with the issues at hand.

> THE AGGRESSOR—This type is very forward and intense and can often overwhelm others by sheer force of how they talk and express themselves. It can be stifling and one sided, which prevents another opinion.

THE PLEASER—Worries more about being liked or making sure that the other person is okay. Can be a pushover and does not say what they may truly feel in order not to cause conflict.

THE ICE HEART/BLACK HEART—(My least favorite) This type reverts to shutting down and being numb. Pretending they don't care and acting like nothing is wrong. Can be very manipulating and cause confusion due to inappropriate reactions in times when deep emotions are present and required.

THE KNOW IT ALL—Has already figured everything out that is "wrong" and has very little respect for another solution or opinion.

THE DENIER/BLAME—Another term you hear often is the "Elephant in the Room". This type often has no interest in acknowledging what the true issue is, won't take any accountability, and often blames others for most issues that arise.

THE VICTIM—Similar to the denier, the victim has an excuse for everything and why it's not their fault.

COMBINATIONS—Getting into an argument can evoke more than one of these reactions and often comes in pairs, or even several of these.

Any of these attributes, if not healed and upgraded, will rarely lead anywhere but to more arguments. Hopefully, understanding different types of responses/reactions will not only help with how to approach the situation better regarding others, but also help you reflect on yourself. The first key to change in any of these is, of course, having the insight and humility to acknowledge you argue in one or several of these manners. Next would be to want to change, knowing it will help make you able to come to authentic compromises and outcomes. It's never easy to admit you have "bad response habits", so being kind and considerate to one another, while working through these types of things is also crucial. Now let's look into some ways to navigate these with the best chances for a mutual understanding and positive change.

HAPPILY, EVER AFTER? (KINDA)

This book is not a fairytale, nor either is life. I wish I could tell you that everything that your ideals envision it to be would manifest, and that, at the end of the rainbow, your treasure awaits. Ironically, the reality is not how or what you want, it only can be what choices you make, especially after love takes an unexpected turn. This is not to say that you cannot salvage something from the occurrence, yet, what you take away, can take a lot of drastic perceptive changing, heartache, confusion, and fear. Your map has been obliterated and your only choice now, as Jordan Peterson likes to say, is to "burn off the deadwood". Who and what you thought you understood about love and relationships has failed and now you must learn again. You must become a novice again; you must be ignorant and at the same time open again. Like a child, you have little to defend yourself with, but only through this mindset will you be able to grow to other states of awareness. Hopefully, doing so with an open and humble heart and without malevolence and bitterness towards the world. And with the hopeful understanding that the "new map" can lead you to a better place, even if just a little better from where you came from.

For me, to heal my relationship by being apart for at least a year (recommended by a therapist and psychologist) versus not having that person at all was my final attempt to allow the river of life to take its course and restore. To hope that we both could heal and come back to a place where a new chapter would commence was the thought. The noble idea that being without someone for as long as it takes, versus not having them at all, was another principle that I had somehow adopted. Sadly, this "principle" was also going to be demolished, as after one year I received no communication. Eighteen months went by, and nothing. Two years, silence. The deafening impact of those two years became a crossroads of sorts. My new map's course had been set and the daunting decision to accept it tormented me. **Choice one** was to continue to hold on to what I knew, what my ideal was and how one day that possibly could be reestablished. This ideal came with a huge cost and at times consisted of insurmountable pain, guilt, and fear, all the while with justification that what "could be" was more important than looking at what actually was. Sometimes the greatest way to say something is to say nothing at all. A lesson I swallowed with angst, sorrow, and resentment. The reality of my life was that she was not coming back, and I was alone… If you would have asked me how I felt about being single prior to this, my first thought would be "I'd deal with it and figure out how to move past it". But the reality of the situation revealed the true character of my inner self. The fact was, I wasn't ready, I had no map, and I began to resort to old habits. The same habits that had gotten me into this situation.

Choice two is the ultimate test of courage and I truly believe, of one's faith. It's looking through life with a new revelation and letting go of all you once defined yourself as. Fortunately for me, there was never any anger or bitterness from my previous relationship, as those emotions, for many, can cause a very justifiable rationale to feel "right". However, I have always wanted to win more than wanted to be right and I had come to the point where staying in the past and trying to stabilize and envision what "could be" was destroying me. I had nothing to lose. I had uncovered every stone, and all that was left for me was to make a new choice. So, that's what I did. At that moment, I decided not to be a victim. I took responsibly for my part, I opened my heart and started looking at how beautiful my life is and committed to unlearning and establishing a new thought system. I relentlessly pushed myself in areas I would never have done before. From going back to school, to what is arguably one of the toughest master's programs in the country, to reading as many books on all the issues I encountered within myself and the previous relationship. I would not settle. I needed to know inside what I could do to be better. Through this process, I began to understand just how much energy I had been suppressing and the results of what that produced were truly remarkable. Instead of sadness and fear of what I had "lost", I became grateful for what I had experienced. That love was never gone, only redirected, and that instead of being my greatest pain, I chose to make her my greatest teacher.
It may not sound like happily ever after and you'd be correct, it was something deeper. It was the ability to love someone that wasn't "there" in the context of how my previous map understood it.

Choice two showed me a different way, a better way, a way to find my why again and to heal my heart. And although I would be lying if I said that there are days, I don't ponder "what could have been" regarding my past love and life, I can honestly say that if I would have not taken the latter option, I may have never made it out. Love is never what we think it should be, but if you truly believe in it, you will do whatever it takes to conquer it. Only then can you understand that it never left you and you were never alone. Don't forget.

CHAPTER 2

FAMILY & MARRIAGE SHOULD BE LIFE GOALS
(Except if you had poor examples growing up, then just getting your shit together should be the goal)

> *"You should want the kind of marriage that makes your kids want to get married."*
>
> —ANONYMOUS

Since family, marriage and love all go hand in hand, piggybacking from the previous chapter only makes sense. The blind assumption that they should be part of your life goals can be a tough pill to swallow **if not deeply analyzed.** One may feel ostracized, if, by the time they reach that "certain age" they are not married with at least one kid, or at least one soon on the way. If this was not challenging enough, the assumption that this can all be done, regardless, if one, or both parties in the relationship, had less than perfect examples of family, really subjects us to some tough lessons and uphill battles. Which begs the question, why do most people so often negate the reality that our examples (or lack thereof) we had growing up, somehow won't be an issue, as we prepare to undertake "until death do us part"?

One of the first justifications we all want to believe is what I covered in Chapter 1. Love can conquer all and will help you get through everything and anything. Another great statement for when the justification for having a child is in question is, "You're never truly ready for kids, it's just something you have to go for." The first of these two ideals tend to get a hall pass, but for me, both have their fallacies, especially having a family "by chance" or the "learning as you go", a rationale that just doesn't seem to be clever or well thought out.

This is not to say that many situations do require we move forward with limited insight. In fact, the more we wait or over-analyze, the higher probability the window for that particular opportunity will close. However, I don't believe that getting married and having a family are something to be rushed. If love indeed conquers all, you need to believe that the time needed, in some regards, may be longer than we initially envisioned. The same goes for bringing a child into the world. Far too many children are being born, for arguably the incorrect reasons.

Relationships are hard. They take work, dedication, patience, and flexibility. Additionally, they take confronting difficult subjects with the full intent of seeing them through until the very end. In those times is when the real work begins and the commitment to one another needs to be tried, tested, and successfully resolved. If you can't get along with your partner's parents or have an abuse or addiction problem, these are just a few examples of major sticking points that may be wise to work out before you commit to anything more serious. It's often the case that the people we are attracted to "fill in" the areas that we lack. While this makes sense and can potentially strengthen the relationship as a whole, unfortunately, many times it just enables the weaker person and distracts us from the necessary work needed to truly feel complete. This makes the consequences of a foundation built on sand much more destructive. The purpose of a healthy relationship starts with two stable people walking together in harmony, not one strong person carrying the other. Yet, the temptation to disregard these issues remains deeply rooted in many people. In my eyes, this is a much more perilous conclusion, one that most people should stop to consider.

So why is the "savior" role in relationships attractive for so many? For me personally I had mastered that responsibility, always taking it upon myself to save the "damsel in distress". Because, well, isn't that what a "strong man" is supposed to do? Bite the bullet and push forward, ignore the warning signs and just muscle through. Signs such as codependency, prior abuse, jealousy, and depression are not to be taken lightly and one way or another, all had been a part of my previous relationships. Consequently, it seemed that the more I chose to carry the relationship, the stronger my partner became, however, by the end, I did not receive nearly as much in return and most of the time I was completely drained. It seems pretty clear that my approach was not working, yet this is all I knew, and all that my current map could provide.

For most, it's easy to play the blame game, but I began to realize that a real "strong man" needed to reflect instead of project. That a real "strong man" had to evolve and embrace the responsibility of why the hero role was not an effective approach. But here was my rub (and maybe the same for others). As men, we instinctually want to be providers, protectors, and leaders. But in an ever "evolving" world where "equality" has become more important than instincts, it blurs the lines. Let me expand. To be strong, you also must be vulnerable and for most men (including myself) the definition of vulnerable tends to fall in the weak category. For most men, learning how to mesh the two has always been a challenge and requires true confidence in yourself and trust in your partner. The old saying that women need to be loved and men respected has never rung truer. In situations like these, the paths and decisions to make can at times seem endless and why bypassing them to dive straight into marriage is often the norm. Indeed, the faith component in a relationship needs to be relevant, listening to your heart is always a good decision, especially if you have an overactive mind. The best bet is to break down your non-negotiables and core values, never yielding to uphold them no matter how good the other person may seem. In the end, when you negotiate these, you both suffer.

Non-negotiables and core values differ for everyone and there are a multitude of factors and life experiences that establish what each person will require and what they cannot negotiate. Regardless, I have found it useful to base these values on the following foundational principles that can be "customized" for your specific needs.

FAITH OR SPIRITUALITY

Although these are in no particular order, one's faith, spirituality or religious beliefs play a major role in the success or failure in a relationship. It's safe to say that for many people, love has no correlation with faith or spiritually and that two people can establish love without the need of either. But, for the others, a large part of how the core of matrimony and the growth of connection are established can be deeply rooted in one's faith or spirituality. Based on this simple understanding, you would assume that having this in common, or not, would be a major topic of contention and unfortunately, no amount of love could change that. It's not to say that faith cannot be adopted, or spirituality meshed with different views and perspectives, but this is one of the main issues, that if not defined from the start, can wedge a major burden on the ability to develop or evolve your relationship. For many, the depth of one's faith not only lies within them as individuals, it also impacts the family dynamic. They say when you marry someone; you marry their family as well, which adds another major consideration as an afterthought.

These are just a few introductory instances that may be a good starting point to diving deeper into the impact that one's faith or lack thereof, can potentially have on your relationship. If you mediate every day at five am but your partner prefers to go to church on Sundays, a question that needs to be asked is, how those two methods can work interchangeably. I don't recommend waiting until after several years in a relationship to start to hash that out. As obvious as it seems, this is more common than not.

FAMILY

Let's say your family is conservative, religious, come from a moderately educated background, upper middle class, well-traveled, cultured, athletic and are entrepreneurs. They are direct speakers, emotionally intelligent, literal and do not condone sarcasm and are very affectionate with one another.

Your partner's family is liberal, not actively religious, also comes from an educated background, middle class, has not gotten out of their city much, let alone visited other countries. They are also athletic and have worked in government or education throughout their entire careers. They are indirect speakers. They lack emotional intelligence and are more focused on themselves than others. They are sarcastic and have a hard time showing any affection.

See any potential complications in this? From the outside, many would immediately be able to identify several and although the literal outlines from this example may be clear, the real world draws people with such opposite backgrounds and far worse, together, more often than you might think. Why is that? Well, for starters, the attributes you lack or may not be intimately familiar with are attractive. "Different" is new, can be exciting, and can even be dangerous. Many people who are too similar rarely gravitate towards one another, as similar strengths can dull one's intrigue and potentially limit the capacity to grow in unfamiliar areas.

This is not to say that contrasting family ideals cannot be dovetailed into a healthy relationship, in fact it's these differences that provide the most growth and challenges to face that prior to the exposure would not have otherwise been possible. There is however a fine line between what constitutes a healthy and achievable balance and when one's need to be aware when "different" turns into toxic. Timeless examples such as the woman who is attracted to the "bad boy", or the man attracted to the "damsel in distress", can be based on unhealthy voids that want to be filled, or are used as distractions from underlining issues. These issues may be subconscious or unresolved. Justifying one's decision to gravitate towards such partners, or falling back into the unhealthy patterns we may have learned from our family.

This makes analyzing the family for both sides of a relationship a critical component. Each situation will have their vast differences and must be approached with that in mind. At the end of the day, you don't need to love each person in your partner's family, in fact, the chances you don't like some of their family members is highly likely. But, if family plays a major role in one or both partners in a relationship, it's wise to determine if the inner workings of how things operate are in line with one another, not to mention the physical and literal requirements some family structures entail. The last thing you want to do is commit to a family who meet once a week, hugs and kisses each other, when your family meets once a year and only cries when someone dies. Set ups like that don't usually go well.

HEALTH & LIFESTYLE

The next topic at hand should come as no surprise, but all too often it is downplayed or overlooked. The lifestyle you have or are envisioning needs to line up with your partner to one extent or another. Although it doesn't mean you both have to run marathons together or partake in the same hobbies, nonetheless, to help ensure sustainability in the relationship, it does mandate that the overall trajectories in how you both live and perceive these topics have some synergy.

What defines "health" can obviously be subjective, but for all intents and purposes let's use a very traditional approach and describe it as the following:

- Engaging in exercise regularly (four-five times a week) either at the gym, running, hiking, group sports, or outdoor activities.

- Eating a diet that consists of very little processed foods, saturated fats, or sugars.

- No drugs and little to no alcohol (perhaps a glass of wine with dinner on occasion).

- Consistent sleep schedule, which includes waking up at the same time even on the weekends.

Many of us don't realize just how important the role of health does play in our lives and when you combine that with another individual, it is at that time you wonder if the blend of what you both define as health is compatible. So, let's say you are an example of the outline just described. It's obvious that discipline and a certain regimen have been established and you might expect that your partner has some, or many of the same habits. However, as time passes, you realize that although certain items you define as "good health" are shared, there are more "unhealthy" habits than you care for. Now why is that important and why should this be addressed sooner rather than later? Mainly because being healthy has a rhythm for each of us and when that is thrown off or altered drastically, it will affect your life. It's okay to enjoy a "cheat day" from time to time and to sleep in after a long week, but beyond that, when others' intentions and dedication differ, the ability to find harmony will show. Scheduling can become a battle. For instance, let's say you are an early riser and like to start your day at the crack of dawn. Before eight in the morning you have already meditated, worked out and eaten breakfast, whereas your partner hits snooze a few times and barely has enough of a window to get ready and dash out to work (missing breakfast and just picking up a cup of coffee on their way). Two very different styles indeed and although the contrast during the week may not be challenging, the weekends, vacations or holidays may not be so simple.

This is where contrasting lifestyles come into play. Again, trying to temper an individual who enjoys filling each day (including weekends) and even when on vacation, enjoys cramming the day with site seeing and excursions, will find life frustrating with someone who likes to sleep in, or lounge around the pool.

The key is balance and respecting that neither one is bad, however, without the foresight to see these situations, and having the expectation that they will just "come around" or "deal with it" is a plan for failure. A good compromise is designating certain trips just for R&R or planning out a mixture of rest and activities. Another idea may be alternating weekends for what each person can tolerate. In the end the most important part is making sure you are able to proceed with one another, but if your health and lifestyles are a constant struggle, better to walk away than try to change someone who doesn't value or understand the same things as you.

CAREER

Work, work, work, work, work. "Honey, you work too much and all you think about is money. I never see you and you're always tired when you get home. When are you ever going to make time for us? There are more important things in life then work, you know. I don't understand why you are so obsessed about a job. Thank God it's Friday. You're not working today are you, it's the weekend?"

Assuming you have to work, one's job or career typically will take up one of the biggest portions of our lives. Knowing this, why would you want to hear constant negative feedback like in the previous paragraph? It's hard enough finding a job we love, or a career we want to pursue, and having the right support system can be one of the biggest deciding factors for sustained happiness and success in a relationship. When you get married and start a family, each person should be very clear on what their careers entail and the commitment and time needed. One of the biggest differences in life is that between an entrepreneur, artist, or athlete, versus someone working a nine-five or more corporate based job. If not tempered and understood early, it can lead to serious unrest. Establishing realistic expectations is a must and from there you can determine if the life you both want to build can line up with the career paths you have chosen. There is nothing worse than one person who loves what they do, having to compromise more than their fair share, with someone who hates their job, or is still searching for their dream career. It can lead to resentment and animosity for both, and even the potential to sabotage each other's drive. That is why it is so important to have your own path and clear objectives for your career. There must be no lack of clarity when it comes to this, especially if there are traditional expectations that require more attention and care in certain areas. Being on the same page with yourself first is truly the only way you can determine if you're ready to have someone walk the path with you.

One of the key factors in a healthy work-life balance is trying to plan out situations and events, versus just deciding on a whim to do something. Of course, everyone loves to be spontaneous from time to time, but as we navigate through our busy lives, forecasting time outside of work and sticking to the commitments often provides the best pathway towards fulfilling those plans. This can help maintain the desires of both people in the relationship and present more balance in each other's work lives. Again, this is a very generic overview and with the understanding that our careers can be much more demanding and that there may be stretches of months or years that limit "balance" with your relationship. This is why it's critical to continuously establish goals and communicate boundaries to see if both sides can support them. Your "whatever it takes" approach of working eighty-hour weeks for ten years straight, versus their forty-hour weeks and weekends-off mindset, may be a compromise that cannot be achieved, and which, can easily derail both of your visions and expectations. Being honest about your careers is a must, especially if you're both just starting out.

MONEY

It's said that money is one of the top deal breakers in a relationship, if not the number one issue. Let's look at some reasons this is often overlooked, and how catching them early can help you determine if your futures can coexist.

Perception and how a person was raised with money is one of the most relative and blatant insights with which to start. Whether someone was brought up poor, middle class, or wealthy, can cause beliefs, expectations and realities to clash. In the world of fantasy, we would all like to believe that "true love" can overpower the social status that money establishes, but this isn't Aladdin (my favorite Disney movie) when the reality is, opposing viewpoints about currency is a surefire path to unrest. Many times, the contrast between rich and poor is much too difficult to bridge and why it's not uncommon for social classes to stick with one another. But for the ones that beg to differ, they must be prepared, for an opposing viewpoint of the value and function of money.

Why? For some, money is the "root of all evil" or a "tool of the devil". For others, money is just an instrument that enables one to live and, in some opportunities, to amass more than others. At the end of the day, money doesn't care how it's made and it's up to the individual to dictate that. Making the money conversation in a relationship a hard one to understand, especially when coming from opposing backgrounds. The Aladdin mention is a classic example of this very topic. Although far-fetched, I don't think that the princess in this story would desire to live on the streets, trying to reestablish her regular lifestyle, no matter how much she loved her hubby.

    Another example where money causes friction is when it's measured or attached to one's self worth. Illustrations such as one member being deemed the "bread winner" of the family, can come with the perception of "higher value" and if not respected and acknowledged can lead to animosity. At the same time, it's the responsibility of the higher earner to be gracious and responsible for the role to which they are committed. Not holding it against their partner and acknowledging the value they bring to the relationship. Ultimately, respect and acceptance can take away the powerful stigmas and emotions money often evokes.

    Whether you're younger and just establishing yourself, or more seasoned in the way of money, when dealing with your partner, it's good to make sure you both have a handle on your finances independently and communicate the difference between wants and needs, saving, investing, and allocating for miscellaneous spending. It is worth considering retaining separate accounts but opening a joint account and having a shared credit card. This is a great way to build trust and understanding of how you both handle money and allows you to adjust as you grow together. What is not wise is to jump into the money world and assume that people look and regard money in the same way you do. Although noble and with good intention, there is nothing worse than couples who jump into finances with the "what's his is mine and what's hers is mine" attitude, only to figure out that his idea of spending an exorbitant amount of money (that took you years to save) on something without your consent is smart to discuss to avoid resentment. As obvious as this sounds, it happens a lot. That is why voicing your concerns, opinions, and boundaries around money is essential before you embark on a serious relationship.

ALCOHOL AND DRUGS

Without getting into the debate about the "health benefits" of certain drugs or alcohol use and assuming we are speaking about this from a recreational purpose outlook, it's safe to say that any excessive use or abuse of either, can or will affect a relationship.

Alcohol and drugs are a major point of contention with the potential to turn a situation bad, quickly, and are always issues to be very clear about from the start. Sometimes the dependence on alcohol and drugs is not so easy to detect and may emerge as the relationship continues. I suggest you make sure you speak about each other's position on both, and it is also highly advisable to discuss each other's families in regard to substance abuse, addictions, and alcoholism. Understanding this can help you gauge things much more realistically and if there are any signs that can be identified. If you or your partner grew up in an alcoholic or addictive family, the chances that you have similar attributes or are more prone to them, are greater. Knowing this is crucial and I believe must be disclosed to one another.

With that said, and assuming you have disclosed your position, if you compromise, it will probably lead to major issues. It's one thing if your significant other enjoys a glass of wine with dinner. It's quite another if they get belligerently drunk and end up praying to the porcelain gods all night. How would you feel if they said, "Hey honey, I'm going out tonight with the fellas to go snort some cocaine. See you when I get back"? Meanwhile, you have never done drugs and don't plan on starting now. Ignoring the signs, or "accepting" these kinds of opposing values will end up costing you the relationship, if not something more serious.

Another challenge is the fact that in many cases our culture continually promotes and glorifies the use of both alcohol and drugs. Making them socially acceptable or legal may make it more "normal" or "cool", however, it does not negate the negative mental, emotional, and physical effects and the consequences each one harbors. Respecting the reality of your personal usage is necessary, and you can then decide if both of your outlooks on alcohol and drugs can be tolerated in your relationship. For some, knowing that these substances have the potential to harm them, put them in states of mind that could also jeopardize their safety, or even possibly kill people, and yet they still proceed, is serious food for thought. Posing the bigger question and subtitle to this chapter, maybe they, or you, need to get your shit together first. It's true that alcohol and drugs are great numbing agents, but you can only run away from your problems for so long. It's also been said that the most difficult things we avoid, or run from, are also the most crucial to make us better people. If you want a family some day or want to improve on what you have, this is not a topic to be skipped.

POLITICS

Over the years and especially recently, the political universe has become much more polarizing and hateful. The mind frame that once was, in that you could agree to disagree, has shifted, and now it's much more "them against us" mentality. It's not uncommon that a discussion in politics can turn into a heated exchange, causing people to damage, or put severe strain on long standing relationships. In addition, one's family upbringing, culture, and history also play a role in an individual's perspectives. Having a clear understanding of one another's stance on these issues is a smart consideration and is not wise to leave it to chance.

So, what's the best course of action to help merge and or better help understand each other's political viewpoints? First and foremost, stick with facts and do your best to truly understand what you are standing for and why. A couple of phrases that really stuck with me during all the mud throwing over the years are "Raise your argument, not your voice" and "Facts don't care about your feelings". Although there is nothing wrong with having passion and wanting to defend your views, to reach any kind of compromise, it's best to have a firm grasp and at least a sound knowledge of the issues and topics. The next big musts are to respect and listen to one another. Assuming that you both can engage in thoughtful exchanges, there may come a point of disagreement. Which, if done with open ears and respect for either side, can help you compromise or at least better appreciate one another's viewpoints.

Finally, unless you are super confident and until you and your partner feel comfortable talking about politics one on one, I've found it's best to limit group conversations, especially with family. Far too often, group discussions can turn emotional and heated, very fast. To be able to agree to disagree and then move on without taking it personally, is a huge advantage in relationships, not only in political exchanges, but in most life lessons.

To minimize or dismiss the impact that each other's political viewpoints can have is a risky line to walk. For some who "doesn't care about politics" or "doesn't know much", it is still a good idea to at least try to understand the difference between major parties and positions if your partner holds strong views. Far too many people let the media indoctrinate them without doing their due diligence, and understanding history gives people the context to think independently. No matter where you and your partner stand, if you can approach your relationship in the same manner, the likelihood that you will be able to coexist happily will be much more attainable.

EDUCATION

This topic is an interesting one and viewpoints vary dramatically. You may ask yourself why it would matter in a relationship. In my experience, the way people value education is a major factor in how you are able to coexist, but most importantly how you are able to grow.

Let's be clear, more education doesn't make you better, in fact, Elon Musk once said, "Don't confuse schooling with education. I didn't go to Harvard, but the people that work for me did". I certainly agree with this and feel that a "higher education" doesn't entitle people to look down on others or think they are better. Far too often it's academics that are unable to mesh wisdom and real-life experiences and exhibit an almost moral high ground, making any kind of authentic exchange virtually impossible. On the flip side, it can be individuals who choose not to educate themselves who base many decisions on emotion and not on facts or reason. I say choose, because in this day and age, education is more accessible than ever before, leaving little excuse for anyone not to educate themselves if they so choose.

So how does this affect your relationship? Again, a good place to start is your partner's family background (see a theme?). You can never underestimate the role a family has in a person's outlook on education, and it's very common to see parallel patterns and traditions of education. More or less education has a significant influence on how a person is raised and dictates a great deal. It is a reasonable place to start and will help you understand where you both stand.

Although there are limitless scenarios, let's use an example of a couple where one person is an entrepreneur, and the person has gone to school for a career that requires a degree (think doctor or lawyer) and why it's important to establish positions on education. With the person who went to school, it's obvious that a major role in their path has been how education has enabled them with their ability to earn a living. Typically, this justifies a high regard for education, and rightfully so. Assuming the entrepreneur did not partake in the "higher education" route (Let's say college degree or further) and worked his or her way up with little schooling, their position on education may not be as prized. To add further layers to the scenario, let's also say that one has achieved higher success in his or her career and the other is just starting out or mediocre at best. Now we are talking! With the outline set, you can see where there may be some potential for disagreement and dispute and can amplify each person's stances on their perceived value of education.

Let's play this out a bit and see what can be done to moderate for the best outcome, or to decide there is not much room for growth. For many people, the definition of "success" differs. But for this example, let's say that the person who is a success has the freedom to travel and purchase just about anything they want. Think of a nice luxury car, a handful of rental properties, eat at nice restaurants whenever they desire, first class flights, etc. They have very limited debt, high income and investments, community recognition that include "best of" awards. Get the picture? It's easy to see that if this person was "highly educated" they could attest to their "success" to their education. However, it's just as fair to say if the person did not go to school and achieved this "success" that they would also have a great argument to discourage or downplay education.

So how could they talk this through? The simple answer would be humility and respect for whatever side the other person is on. But a deeper suggestion may be to realize that there is no "right way" to attain education and that either path, in many instances, may be just as, or more effective. Historically, both have shown to produce dynamic results and actually hold a lot more in common than you may think. Instead of getting caught up in who has the MBA or PhD or who made more money, finding the value in one another's perspectives and how their paths helped them is a much more productive approach. At the end of the day, there are very few people who become successful without educating themselves in one way or another, just because they don't approach it the same way, doesn't discredit them. Maintaining that kind of perspective can be very useful when you come to a disagreement.

Unfortunately, it's not always as easy to have that perspective and some hurdles cannot be overcome. If the person you are with has no desire to grow their knowledge, this is a red flag. Because ultimately the person who is always educating themselves, will more than likely outgrow the other. Making it very challenging to have things in common and the ability to relate. It's another red flag if a person is judgmental and thinks they are "better" with education, or discredits education in the same vein. If mutual respect is not found, you cannot have a healthy relationship. You also cannot force people to embrace education, so it may be better to move on.

Learning and education is a lifelong endeavor and is a key to a healthy, sustaining and stimulating relationship. It doesn't mean that everyone needs to be a bookworm, but it also doesn't mean that you can justifiably excuse yourself completely and expect to maintain higher and deeper levels that a healthy relationship demands. Taking this topic into consideration is a way to grow and maximize each other.

PERSONALITIES

Opposites attract. Good girls often like bad boys. Her strength is my weakness. We have all heard these statements and each one can hold some truth. Meeting someone who holds counter attributes to your own can be captivating. In fact, the intrigue can even hold a feeling of mystery or danger. Things that aren't familiar can lead to attraction. However, once the dust settles and you digest the reality, it's necessary to consider personality traits and if the contrasts enable you to coexist.

Let use the classic examples of the "bad boy" and "princess" personalities. One is defined as a loner and rebel, someone who doesn't follow the rules, lives in the "grey area" of life, "rides the line" and has no problem imposing his will in any situation. Now our princess couldn't be more different. She enjoys following all the rules, looks at life as black and white, dislikes risk and prefers stability and consistency and only speaks up when the situation deems it appropriate, even if that means biting her tongue. Based on both of these personality traits, you could have an argument for both sides, on why personalities like these are attracted to one another or not, as well as the consequences if they decide to give it a go. So, let's look at some potential pros and cons and why they should consider being honest about one another's personalities.

The obvious "pro" is the balance that two contrasting personalities can provide. One of the main reasons people don't like to date, or marry someone who is too similar, is that things can become stale. Whereas the contrast of different personalities can keep things exciting and fresh, offering a broader perspective across the relationship. Let's say you are more of an introvert and prefer to stay at home during the weekend, however your partner is more extroverted and enjoys concerts, hikes, or road trips. Both provide great options if able to find the balance that both partners need, and can be a harmonious dance that complement each other quite well. On the flip side, if one personality runs the show, it can have harsh consequences and lead to a grueling scenario. An example is when one partner gravitates towards being around family, while the other has a limited desire to do so, and eventually, they stop trying. Over time, a resentment builds and in this can cause a major rift or inability to compromise.

Both these simple examples show why it is wise to be clear on each other's personalities. What starts out as "cute" or "sexy" quickly turns into exactly what derails the relationship. There is nothing wrong with having a degree of contrast, however many relationships run into problems when the "ideal" of what you think or want someone to be, negates the truth of who the person truly is. It's your responsibility to be honest with yourself and make sure you can handle the other's personality. Too many times we try to compartmentalize each other and then, when the personality trait you least like emerges, it shakes the whole foundation. Accepting someone's core personality traits is key and knowing what you can and cannot tolerate should be established early on. Otherwise, it can lead to an array of resentment and confusion, having your partner thinking you were always "okay" with his or her key personality traits, only to discover they were just being tolerated or even ignored.

It's not to say people cannot or should not compromise or do their best to adjust. However, to expect someone to change completely is not fair for either person. Know your limits, versus expecting the other person to yield to your desires. Again, there is always give and take, but I recommend you assess your ability to handle contrasting personality traits.

AGE

The last topic of this chapter has many perspectives and if we consider it from a cultural viewpoint, it can get very broad. Personally, and as a descendent of Mexican heritage, it's not uncommon for the culture to marry and have a family at a young age. But to make this more universal, I will share examples based on a general western philosophy and culture. This also has its sticking points, but the goal is to help you outline the pros and cons of age regarding a relationship. Individuals have their preferences to date, love and marry whomever they choose, and age is a part of that assuming legal age laws are followed.

The obvious issues that age plays in any relationship need to be analyzed just like any other topic. From, generational differences, stages in life, to biology, being aware of how age plays a part in a relationship is often overlooked.

If you are in a relationship with someone similar in age, many things we may not think about or take for granted, are simplified right off the bat. Although you may have different likes and dislikes and a range of other individual perspectives, the general core baselines are much more relevant and established. The first example we can use is generational experiences. Let's say, you both grew up in Generation X (those born between mid-sixties to early eighties). The shared age range provides great potential to relate and and grow from similarities. From cartoons, music, movies, history, sports, whatever the topic, you both had many of the same input during the same times.

The next example, "stages of life", will also be parallel. If you are both just out of college and establishing yourself in life and the work force, it makes the context of the relationship familiar and arguably easier to grow and share.

The final example of biology can be very broad, so to keep this simple and without getting into moral or religious debates, let's set the example of a healthy childless couple under the age of 30. With the stage set, a couple venturing into starting a family can hope for a successful pregnancy, a healthy child, and the ability to maintain sustained energy levels while raising their child.

Now let's widen the age difference and see why age needs to be acknowledged in any relationship. The male in the relationship is 50 and the female is 28. It's clear that the first example of generational experiences, will not be shared. While the 28-year-old was going through high school, the 50-year-old would have been already advanced well into his life and career.. This is not to say that a bridge cannot be built, but the challenges to relate and connect, will be more apparent, and similarities due to their age will be reduced.

The next example is "stages of life". At 28 you can argue that the female is in the early stages of life, with not much work, or life experience compared to the 50-year-old, whereas the 50-year-old is arguably halfway through his life. This could include a past marriage and family, an established career, potential for loss and other life experiences that a longer life naturally delivers.

These are all generalized assumptions, as one can argue, each of the "experiences" for both age groups, but for the sake of examining why age should be considered while establishing your relationship, I found it best to outline a scenario under these models. The 28-year-old might be the man and the 50-year-old the women. Which in the first two examples would be easily exchangeable, however, when we get into the final example of biology, it's when gender and age play an undeniable role. Keeping the model the same (28-year-old female and 50-year-old male) let's assume children are being discussed. From a biological standpoint, a 50-year-old raising a family versus a 28-year-old clearly poses challenges. The first thing that comes to mind is energy. At 28 you can assume you will have more compared to the 50-year-old. As time passes and the child ages, so will the 50-year-old. Although they may be able to mentally keep up with the child, physically it could be more challenging. Let's say 16 years pass and your child is engaged in physically challenging sports (Basketball, tennis, martial arts). Now at 66 and assuming the person is in good health, even so, when compared to the 44-year-old, there is justification to believe it will be more physically challenging and demanding for the 66-year-old.

Now let's flip this yet again. With the 50-year-old being the women and the 28-year-old being the man. Some of the biggest hurdles a women faces are due to her biological clock and the inherent risk factors that come with "older mothers". When compared to a man, except for the inability to not have children at all, he has little to no risk. That is why I recommend you consider age in a relationship no matter whether you're a man or a woman.

For many, not looking at these factors for the sake of love, is a risky choice. But for those who are clear on the challenges imposed by age differences but are still willing to proceed, I don't see anything wrong in it. Some argue that older parents are selfish because of the risk it poses to the child and the restrictions older age brings in raising children, but ultimately if the risks are acknowledged and accepted, then I believe we are free to date, marry, love, and raise a family with anyone we want. There is no right or wrong age range, and any scenario will always have its issues.

CONCLUSION

Getting married and having a family can be one of the most profound and life altering things we do as human beings. To find harmony with another person and to be able to grow and maintain it, is no doubt something that most of us have considered and possibly desired. But like anything great, it takes a ton of work, sacrifice and commitment and unfortunately many of us fail to look at, accept, acknowledge or understand the details. It is my intention that the lists and simple examples I provided will be a guide to help you prepare or expand on issues you may be encountering.

Family & marriage should be life goals, except if you had poor examples growing up, then just getting your shit together should be the goal. Hopefully this chapter will help you with all that.

CHAPTER 3

TIME HEALS EVERYTHING
*(Except if you don't work on the issues,
or live in denial and distractions)*

*"We cannot begin again
We cannot make a new start as though the past has not passed
But we can plant something new
In the burnt ground
In time we will harvest a new story of who we are
We will
Build a relationship that is tempered by the fire of our history
You are a person who has hurt me
I am a person who has hurt you
And knowing those truths we choose to make something new
Forgiveness is my back bent to clear away the dead tangle of hurt
And recrimination
And make a space, a field fit for planting
When I stand to survey this place, I can choose to invite
You in to sow seeds for a different harvest
Or I can choose to let you go
And let that field lie fallow"*

—DESMOND TUTU

Time heals everything. In some regard truth can be found in this statement, but for most of us, holding on to our past can often dictate our present, which can ultimately define our future. The greatest way to measure time is through action, and only through action can you ever create the opportunity to heal. At first, no action, or living in denial or distraction may be necessary to cope. But to stay in any one of these states for a prolonged period, shows that, as time continues to pass, you are still stuck. As difficult as it may be to persevere, what is the hardest part to accept is that staying stuck is always a choice, and not only a choice, but YOUR choice. Let's expand and use a failed relationship as the example.

After taking action, one of the most crucial steps in healing is self-accountability and reflection. It's easy to blame another person. It's easy to stay the victim, and it's easy to stay in an ivory tower of self-righteousness, hurling down what could be endless accusations of the other person's faults and shortcomings. Even if they are true. He cheated on me; she drank too much and couldn't connect; she disrespected my family; he worked too much, or whatever the issues… Until you are ready to look at your role in the situation, nothing will change. Blaming someone doesn't change that you are still stuck and getting unstuck and healing should be the number one goal. Making "them understand" won't ever change what happened and we are often caught in a vicious cycle of wanting to show them what they did, versus looking at ourselves and what we did or did not do. For anyone to think they played no role in the undoing of any relationship, is truly a narcissistic and self-righteous stance. No one is perfect, and until you decide to reflect on what part you played, you will stay stuck. Without this acknowledgment and reflection, people can stay trapped in the past forever and carry the pain into other areas and relationships throughout their lives.

One of the major traps of the refusal to be accountable is when we start making our opinions on the issues that caused the split more severe than the other persons. This again justifies our "position" and gives no opportunity for the other to ever be excused, but more importantly, for you to never justify forgiveness (more on this later). It's not to say that each person's core values of what they will and will not put up with don't matter. In fact, for any healthy person, having clear boundaries is crucial. However, it also doesn't mean that if your "number one" deal breaker in a relationship, is say, cheating and the other person's is lack of connection, that yours, or theirs, are any less significant. This again shows why establishing these issues, as outlined in Chapter 2, is a good idea. So how do you free yourself?

Quite simply, you must focus on what you may have missed, overlooked, ignored, or denied. And although you may never know exactly "why" something didn't pan out the way you envisioned, your willingness to reflect on yourself will strengthen your ability to be better in the future and hopefully avoid similar mistakes. But how do you do that? In my experience, seeking the information that you lacked, and leaving **no stone unturned,** is the first step to healing.

Reading everything I could put my hands on and listening to podcasts on subjects I did not understand was a major tool for me. Many times, during the "mud throwing" of a breakup, we are labeled or judged in a way in which we may not be familiar. Accusations such as, "You're a narcissist" or "You can't ever understand what it's like to be raised and abandoned by addicts", can be shocking when you're unprepared for them. Instead of just accepting statements,

I found that tackling them from top to bottom empowered me and ultimately enlightened me on truths, and debunked the untruths. (I was relieved to discover that I'm not a narcissist, but may be a bit on the hypomanic side!) What we cannot face on our own, we should speak to a professional about. Of course, friends and family can be useful to some degree, but we also need a third-party individual who is unbiased and trained in the methods to help us see what we need to, not what we want to.

Finally, after all the work is done and you feel confident, you've understood your role in the relationship's outcome, you are now equipped to forgive and let go.

Forgive and let go. It sounds simple and easy to understand. But the reality is far from easy and the patterns we fall into when analyzing situations regarding painful experiences can be all-consuming and never-ending. Time truly becomes irrelevant when the mind is stuck in a loop. Lifetimes can be lost when we're trapped in denial, anger, heartbreak, pain, **and whys.** Some of the worst periods in my life were when I became stuck in the "why". Why did this happen? Why didn't this work? Why did this fail? Why didn't I do that? Why did I do this? Even worse, is trying to understand another's why. Why didn't they understand me? Why couldn't they connect? Why did they drink? Why did they cheat? Even if you are sure you know why, it's difficult to accept when it hurts.

The good news is that there is a map to guide you out of the "why trap", and over time, if you are open and accepting, your ability to heal will manifest. Let's start with the first group of whys that I outlined that are about you and the relationship as a whole:

Why did I do this? Or why didn't I do that? The fact is, if you look deeper into any situation without pointing the finger at anyone, the answer will be revealed. Often, in approaching the situation like this, the bigger truth may be that you don't like what you will discover and what you have buried inside, and deep down you already knew. That is why accepting truthful answers is much tougher than blaming others. With blame and judgment, we have a free pass to not look at ourselves and it may seem like it works, but time will reveal it as only a quick fix at best.

Once the truthful answer has come to light and been totally accepted, you can then let it go. It will never change what has happened. You may never get an apology or be able to apologize. It may never change the other person's role or understanding, and it may not enable you to be in that person's life anymore. But it can give you a clear acceptance of an outcome so you will no longer be stuck. It will also often require you to look at the role you played in the situation, even if you were on the "receiving end". If accepted and embraced, this can be a great tool and opportunity to grow and learn from the lesson. These are the only "whys" you can "control". These whys are within yourself and through hard work, forgiveness, love, and acceptance, you will prevail. Beyond that and regarding the **other person's why,** this is where it ends. Let's discuss that next.

The other person's "why" is a dangerous and slippery slope and ultimately if not touched upon with caution, can lead to endless confusion, resentment, pain and suffering. Thankfully, we cannot control another person's choices. Far too many times, we bring the other person into our thought system, which utterly takes away from our ability to heal and forgive. In my situation, it did not matter how many times an explanation was given, or how many times I tried to understand why things in my relationship regarding the specific actions failed. It was only until I looked at my part and what enabled me to take responsibility that I could heal. It's not to say that I did not analyze both sides and take a deep look at the situation, however after a while, I became more consumed with trying to understand the other person than in trying to accept reality.

In life, there will be many times when you don't get the answers you want. It is in those times where you need to be honest and at peace with the work you have done on yourself in establishing your "whys". Otherwise, you get lost in assumptions and scenarios about the other person, even taking it as far as blaming yourself for "could haves" or "should haves". Although it's a noble ideal and good to be accountable and aware, it will only serve you for a limited time. We are all humans, we all make mistakes and will continue to make mistakes. It does not justify a wrongful act but dwelling on "should & could haves" over an extended period of time is like beating a dead horse. Many times, we also shift the blame because we don't want to hold the other person accountable.

In every relationship, each side needs to be aware of his or her role; bad outcomes rarely happen overnight and being truthful about actions you may have underplayed, discredited, or even ignored helps balance your ability to see things more clearly.

STILL STUCK? Speaking from experience, there are those of us who believe they are beyond stuck and no matter how much time passes, we just can't get over the sorrow. The pain and inability to move beyond broken dreams and unfulfilled expectations, at times, seem unbearable. Personally, I would feel like I had made significant progress and healed a great deal, only to be thrown back into such deep pain that felt like I had not moved an inch. It was like the analogy of a hydra; I would overcome one issue and two more would seem to appear.

So, what can you do after you have "done the work", put forth the effort and committed to being in the moment and not living in denial and distractions, and yet you cannot seem to get over it? For me, the key was always unrelenting action and the commitment to never quit. Pushing harder no matter what the obstacle was, believing that at the end of my efforts based on pure will alone, that my rewards would await at the finish line. And for the majority of the time, this was the map that led me to achieving what I wanted. But unfortunately, the more books I read, the more effort I obsessively dedicated, and the more I looked at myself, the more complete healing still eluded me. After so much time studying and doing the work, my mind was crystal clear and understood why my relationship had failed, but that wasn't the problem. The problem was my heart. **And no amount of reading can ever cure a broken heart** (Trust me, I read a lot!).

Again, my map had run out of directions and the "formula" for answers had no clear distinctions. Options were limited, and at this point it was crucial I make the correct decision. The first option I had was to go back to what I knew. Old habits die hard, and the comfort of the past tends to embrace us more, especially when we are stuck floating in the wind. However, the pain I had endured was impactful enough for me to pass on that option.

I was tired of doing the same stuff and crucially; I was **willing** to change. Option two was to continue seeking—hoping the next book, podcast, or therapy session would reveal what I needed to finally heal. And although I will never stop learning and I understand the great utility of this approach, I was clear that I had exhausted this method.

The final step for my healing was arguably the most challenging. It required me to stop my old habits and stop force-feeding myself "self-help". So, what was left, you ask?

For me, it was giving the relationship back to God.

CHAPTER 4

IT'S BEST TO WAIT TO HAVE SEX UNTIL YOU'RE MARRIED
(Except for the people who don't wait)

*"Our need for togetherness exists alongside
our need for separateness."*
—ESTHER PEREL

In today's world and culture, it is nearly impossible to avoid the constant bombardment of sex. From social media, news, music, sports and anything else you can think of, the saturation of the hypersexual era seems to be more mainstream and normalized each passing day. The days of the modest and discrete have been replaced by little to no regard for others and are capped off by an almost villainized perspective if you don't choose to embrace others' sexual preferences and beliefs. As ridiculous as it sounds, what you have (or don't have between your legs) is assumed to be a rite of passage that everyone must not only be okay with, but happily accept with no room for debate. It's not hard to understand why the time when people's biggest concern was sex before marriage, has been replaced with WAP (look it up and you'll understand), and other, in your face overtly sexual messages, that rule the airways and media. The fact that this type of promotion is not only being entertained, but aggressively promoted and accepted is an unnerving thought. And even more concerning to me are the people being shunned, when all they want is not to have to hear others openly promote their sexual endeavors or preferences. **So why is this an untruth?**

The depth that sex plays in our lives is obviously highly influenced by our surroundings. What we see each day and what is fed into our mind, can typically reveal trends. But the embedded instincts with which we are predisposed, are often the leading and driving force. With these two energies at work, it is not surprising that such hypersexual developments are having arguably unforeseen impacts, making "truths" and "norms" of sex **a struggle** and people feeling like they have to fight between their mind, heart, soul, and genitals!

The reality is that sex in our society has become all too commonplace. The sacred act of humans engaging with each other, now seems to be no less private or important, than using the bathroom. Emphasizing more on who—who is next, and how many? Today's media has no qualms about making idols and sex symbols out of past and present celebrities, whose sexual exploits (the more explicit the better tends to be the theme) outweigh anything and everything. This attitude just affirms "normalcy" in these kinds of behaviors, without truly investigating the repercussions of what these "trends" do to the perspective of sex in our society. I recently saw an article about a celebrity couple who split up after a long marriage and within weeks both had "replaced" each other with someone new. The media was more interested in who the "new people" were, than the fact that their divorces hadn't even gone through before each person had moved on to the next partner.

CHAPTER 4—IT'S BEST TO WAIT TO HAVE SEX UNTIL YOU'RE MARRIED

Although promiscuity has been around for as long as the human race, the change in how sex is being openly promoted and expressed, does not appear to be trending in the correct direction for our mental, emotional, and spiritual well-being. Like it or not, sex binds us in the most intimate manner. As much as people want to think that they can behave casually when engaging in sex, it's just not sustainable, especially as a lifestyle. What separates us from animals is our ability to connect and love. Sex plays a major role in some relationships, and can increase vulnerability, openness, desire, trust, depth, and unity. But when that is downplayed and replaced by pure instinct and desire, the ability to truly connect lessens and people can become numb; always chasing a feeling for the next high to fill the bottomless void.

Another huge impact on sex is the porn industry. With little to no restrictions, and available wherever there is internet, porn often depicts perverse sex for all genders and affiliations. At the touch of our fingertips, we now have access to watch more sex than ever before. And although some porn can be utilized as part of an exploratory and diverse way to expand sexuality, the excess and often degrading production of the current porn industry, typically leaves little room for imagination and can even be deeply degrading with arguably toxic sexual depictions. This can lead to a wildly unrealistic mindset for both men and women and distorts the ability to develop a healthy understanding of sex.

From body image, sexual expectations, and the number of sexual partners, the expectations that porn encourages when seen as a comparison to everyday sexual activity is a dangerous phenomenon that is becoming all too common. Porn can also make people lazy. Why chance the possibility of rejection, when you can satisfy your desires with porn? It's fast, easy and enables the broadest of fantasies, with the most "beautiful" people, without any of the pitfalls of actually engaging in real life sex. Soon it can become the rule, versus the exception, with no reason to veer from this pattern. I believe porn puts unreasonable pressure on both sexes for "how" sex should be and what kind of sex "should be" expected. For many of us, sharing sex with someone is an evolving and maturing experience. The more comfortable and familiar you get with somebody, hopefully the better understanding you have of each other's sexual desires. It's not realistic to think that right out of the gate, you or your partner will have the understanding, confidence, or even the desire to challenge the abilities of a full-fledged porn actor. At times, this can make the anticipation of sex more nerve-racking than the act itself. The problem with porn is that it leaves little to the imagination, and because of that, has the ability to dilute the experience, or worse, have people continuously striving for what many consider unrealistic sexual experiences.

Dopamine, which is a chemical released in the brain that makes you feel good, also plays a continual role in sex, and like any other stimulant, if overdone, can end up being an addiction versus a natural experience. For the small percentage of individuals who partake in this kind of behavior, once reduced or stopped, it makes it difficult to enjoy anything but the "extremities". This can make it very difficult to reintegrate into a healthy relationship and often keep one ostracized until balance is restored. The true experience of sex and intimacy is much deeper than what porn depicts, making it crucial to acknowledge what porn is and more importantly what it is not. We must have a healthy balance in how we frame our thought system around sex.

The duality that sex plays in our culture can, at times, be a very difficult standard to achieve and maintain. Men are often glorified for their number of sexual conquests and women shunned for exactly the same. The irony is that when these desires are "fulfilled" by men, they typically are left not only feeling empty, but at times confused by the "lack of" or "what should have been", after the deeds are accomplished. The same goes for women, who may feel and think that partaking in the same activity as men will somehow "liberate" them through the fallacies that tend to follow promiscuity. Yet again, it often leaves them feeling hollow, and more trapped than before. And although the "humans are animals" and have "desires" argument, will no doubt always be made, far too many times these actions appear to cause an opposite reaction and leave us longing for something deeper.

For me personally that was exactly the case; the longing for more than just the casual rendezvous, or "something to do" that I had long been accustomed to. But from an early age and from my cultural experiences, I found myself defending "my right" to do as I pleased. And without a strong guide or influence to emulate when I did run into issues, I spent many years repeating hopeless habits, thinking "the next one" would settle me down, using one sexual encounter after another to justify my mindset. The hard truth was that my map had failed me and there was nowhere left to turn. The duality of the instant pleasure that was produced by being promiscuous, and the outward "praise" that was clearly reinforced and accepted, versus the almost instant lack of desire to go any further after sex, continuously battled within me. In my mind, I knew that sex and intimacy were party to each other, and almost indistinguishable when encompassed in a healthy manner. But in reality, I was using sex to distract from other issues and to make myself feel better. Giving up something that was socially accepted, easy for me to achieve, and getting constant positive reinforcement and, of course, pleasure, was the perfect recipe for a vicious cycle. Unfortunately, it wasn't until I hit a major wall that it finally registered, and as a consequence, I ended up hurting others and myself, more than I could have ever imagined.

When the dust had settled, I was shattered, broken, and in pieces. My intentions although pure of heart, had been overtaken by the "untruth" in my mind. I realized that sex was not something to be taken lightly and was not just a physical act. If engaged upon, you must be willing to deal with all the consequences that follow, such as mental, emotional, physical, and spiritual. In the past, I would supplement what was not working or "missing" in the relationship. And instead of dealing with the main issue at hand, I took the easy route, ignored the problem, while trying to cover it up with excuses and justifications. From the outside looking in it's astonishing that somewhere in my mind I thought I could ride it out. Only to have the house come crashing down and no one to blame for my actions but myself. If I was stronger, and had my map been better, I would have dealt with the core issues. But my fear about the likelihood of dealing with the real issues, and then not succeeding, scared me more than infidelity. Making it worse, losing my integrity and the ability to defend my true feelings to the person I only wanted to love.

I had become the bad guy; I had taken the easy path, and in doing so, gave her the excuse not to examine herself, but to blame me for the entire relationship breakdown. My actions had again led me to a dead end and required me to shift. And the only way that was going to happen was if I looked within to what I truly wanted, versus the ideal I had manifested.

CHAPTER 4—IT'S BEST TO WAIT TO HAVE SEX UNTIL YOU'RE MARRIED

Sex in many cultures and throughout history has typically been a private matter, many times considered taboo and often peppered with specific traditions, demands and expectations. And although there are numerous guidelines provided for our spiritual, mental, emotional, and physical well-being, sometimes the "modern human" cannot meet the demands of the current day terrain. The examples of this could be a book in itself, so instead of going down that path, the course I took to help build a new and better map to follow, was to identify what I felt were the non-negotiables. (I did this based on a western philosophy, as there are vast cultures that accept multiple wives and countless other things that would be polar opposite when compared). And although it is certain that each person's "list of rules" will be unique, my intention is to give you a template that you can customize, to define what sexual non-negotiables mean for you. Doing this will hopefully give you a better outlook on your desires, wants and needs and put things into perspective, versus trying to be everything for your partner, when in reality your list may not make that possible.

SEX RULES!

RULE 1—*Sex is Deeper Than Just the Physical*

Sex is a powerful act and has much utility—not only physically, but mentally and emotionally too. It requires trust, compassion, vulnerability, intimacy and is one of the first major steps to establishing true connection and love. Let's face it, some of us are more sexual than others and that's okay. However, a major component for success is making sure all parties are clear on their intentions, boundaries and expectations and leaving nothing up for assumption. Too often, we assume that because we have connected through sex, everything else becomes clear for both people. When in fact, it may be the opposite and leaves us more unsure about what the next steps are or should be, especially if we jumped into bed quickly. For those that discard or under emphasize the act of sex as "just an action" or "being horny", risk a shallow lifestyle and, as a consequence, end up hurting others, and often pervert their own ability to love on a deeper level.

Half of my family come from Mexican origins, and it was not uncommon for this side of my family to start having children very young and to promote sex and promiscuous behavior. I'll never forget, I took my "non-Latin" and very American girlfriend I was dating at the time, to my eighty-year-old grandmother's house. During the visit she openly stated "My hito (my son in Spanish) you're such a handsome man, and have such a beautiful lady, but make sure you spread that to as many beautiful women as you can!" Needless to say, that was not taken too well by my lady and I had to spend quite some time explaining what grandma "meant" and why culturally, sex was perceived differently than in American culture. This is just one example of my specific situation, which can clearly result in contrasting viewpoints and behaviors regarding sex in relationships and why understanding the depth of how we all personally regard and define sex is necessary. Sex is a very intimate and personal issue and although culture, religion, and upbringings can help you with some forms of expectations, it's never enough to assume anyone thinks or feels a certain way. The only way to be sure is to ask and engage and as the relationships grows, to make the topic of sex just as important as all the other major components that make a relationship work.

Although sex and attraction are a key indicator and a vital necessity, it is only one step to determining compatibility. The fact that engaging in sex "connects" us for that moment doesn't always mean it will sustain us, and far too often, we base our initial interpretation of sexual intimacy as the frontrunner for defining love. This is even more emphasized if the sex is "good" and can also often be misinterpreted. Few will dispute the thrill that a passion filled rendezvous can provide, but the problems unfold when hollow sexual experiences lose their "buzz" quickly and reality sets in. This is especially the case if a deeper relationship has not been established, giving neither person any real incentive to continue and often ending faster than it started. This type of behavior, if not acknowledged, becomes more instilled and people end up jumping from one sexual partner to the next. This leaves many wondering why a true connection was not established, why nothing came out of the situation after sex, and it makes the possibility of a richer and more fulfilling relationship much more challenging.

Understanding that anytime you engage in sex with someone you are creating a connection, not just physically, but emotionally, mentally, and for many, spiritually, needs to be at the forefront of your mind if you want to go beyond the physical. The difference between us and animals is our ability to be intimate with one another beyond the justification for procreating and survival. And as much as we might like to think we can detach the act of sex from our feelings, it's just not the case. Trust me, I know from experience. In the end, many of us desire not only the physical joy that sex provides, but the multitude of other opportunities it can create with another person. And as much as many people try to deny this, it's only when we take responsibility for the role sex plays in our life, that we can truly acknowledge the depth of its meaning, which is far greater than we may realise.

RULE 2—*Sexual Desires and Expectations Should Be Talked About, Not Assumed*

We all know that the anticipation and the fantasy of sex have as much of an impact, if not more so, than the act itself. This, of course, can be a double-edged sword if the reality does not deliver our fantasy and our expectations are not met. And it's even more of an issue if you or your partner don't share your innermost thoughts. In many circumstances, our ability, or our partner's ability, to say what we desire or don't desire, is challenging. And if it is not expressed correctly, it can lead to a buildup frustration and animosity. This is again, why understanding how and what you both want, must be established and shared. Only then can you determine if you are able to oblige one another and or shift and grow in a realistic and healthy manner for both of you.

Personally, I live in my mind as much as in my body, if not more. Meaning, if there was a fight or disagreement and things are not good with me and my partner, the last thing I want to do is engage in sex. But many like to bypass the issues and jump right into the physical, hoping it will lead to a better outcome. For me, there is nothing wrong with "make up sex", but only after the main points of contention have been ironed out. This specific topic was something that took me a while to figure out and I could not express it articulately, which ultimately led to more problems down the road. My partner thought that sex could "cure" the issue, but I wasn't open enough to say how I truly felt. She thought that for me "as the man" this should be the answer and all else would be healed and restored. Only after years of me not saying anything, but each time being less and less engaged, did it then become clear to her that "something" was not right. That conversation was harder than I anticipated. Having to reassure her she was not the issue and that it was my reluctance to say how I felt and what I needed, and that I was stuck in my mind. From there, it did not get any easier, because for so long, the opposite was enabled and had been deemed a "positive" feedback loop. All the while, I tried to ignore my feelings and opted not to express the difficulties I felt each time we had sex after a fight.

The point that is crucial to take away from Rule 2 is why sharing what you are thinking can make or break your relationship, and the longer you wait, the more you risk being unable to shift things to a healthy state. It comes down to being honest with yourself and, in turn, giving your partner the ability to decide how, or if, they can adjust. This is why for many of us (myself included) it's "easier" (or so we think) to swallow our desires, and not disturb, or rock the other person's boat. The intention is that "my stuff" is not a big deal and can easily take a back seat. Of course, each person has to determine and decide what is appropriate and not petty. Because in the end, it's better to face the consequences and the truthful outcome of your partner's decisions, than to stay stuck in your mind and build a false sense of reality, which will often lead to an unsatisfactory conclusion.

RULE 3—*After Sex The Real Work Starts*
In a new and blooming relationship, the physical universe tends to be the focal point and enable some of the most intense physical components of the initial connection.

Assuming you have established a healthy sex life and have a good understanding of each other's intimacies and hopefully you both are satisfied and consistently enjoying the endorphins. So now what? If you're like most of us, the challenges of the post sex realities are no joke and require consistent and creative efforts on both sides. As the honeymoon stage shifts and the relationship enters a new chapter, the realization that, what is between your legs can only get you so far, forces us to become more aware of our partner's needs beyond the bedroom.

As a relationship gets longer, this becomes especially true, and if not addressed, can result in two people having very little understanding of how to further stimulate and challenge one another beyond sex. In turn, other areas of your relationship can stagnate. Your sex life can also get affected, leaving you with even less connection. I recommend you address the point of this rule and why the real work must now begin.

So, what is "real work"? In my experience it can range from a thoughtful home prepared dinner, a walk at the park, a voicemail saying you love them and are thinking about them, a bouquet of flowers, or even an unexpected hug or kiss during the "routine" times in life. The what pales in comparison to the why, making it never a bad time to tell, or show the person you love, that you love them. The key is to do it **consistently** and especially when they may need it more than you, or when you may not necessarily "have to" do anything or want to, but are willing to work for what you want. Which ideally is a healthy, intimate, and long-lasting relationship.

Far too often, we get caught in our ruts and forget about others. But if you're willing to **put in the work** and show creativity for one another, it will often reward you in ways beyond what you can imagine. Frequently, this "work" turns out not only to provide more depth and meaning, but is the spark that continually reignites the romance and sexual desires back into play. Turning your "work" into a perfect segue to light the fire for one another and create the balance with sex once again.

RULE 4—*Sex Should Be A Joyous Act, Not A Pressure Filled Obligation*

In this day and age and when compared to historical times, sex has arguably become much more "mainstream", liberal and socially acceptable. The days of modesty in many regards have long passed, and the assumed future of the boundaries of sex truly is hard to fathom. In some ways, the aggressive nature of the "freedom" to express one's sexuality has its good attributes. However, like many movements, this trend is also detrimental to the fundamentals of sex, and stacks enormous social pressures and unrealistic expectations on both males and females alike. Where once being a joy and relief, for many, now has become a subset of prerequisites, comparisons, and standards, that often overshadow the act of sex itself. Let me expand.

UP TO HERE

The problem when sex becomes more mainstream and less private begins when we compare ourselves to others. With the online saturation of social media, it's far too easy to become overwhelmed with the constant "ideal images", situations and or expectations that are endlessly depicted. We forget that many of the images are rehearsed, planned, edited and completed only after multiple takes! For the vast majority, our sex lives are more spontaneous than strategic. However, the issue remains that many men and women now face higher anxiety and stress because of the pressures of what they feel they "should be". It's great to look nice for your partner and make a genuine effort, but when the desire to "have to look a certain way" or put your expectations onto your partner based on unrealistic comparisons, that it can become a problem. Which, in turn, completely takes the joy and excitement out of what sex should encompass.

In my opinion, some of the best sexual encounters or exchanges are unplanned, and, for good reason, sex should require a level of trust and comfort and is a natural part of a healthy relationship. If you or your partner always have to be prepared or are always anticipating, versus relaxing and letting things happen, it puts far too much pressure on both people, especially when it doesn't happen when you expect it. The best solution is approaching sex as a natural and beautiful act of love, trust and connection and being okay with things not being in your control all the time. Plan when you can, and for special occasions, but beyond that, letting go of comparisons will be a significant step toward a more fulfilling and exciting sex life.

RULE 5—*Sex Changes With Age*
As the relationship grows and develops, your sex life will inevitably change. Again, for each person and relationship, this will be unique. However, for everyone, I think it's safe to say that their experience of sex at the start of a relationship, versus a couple of years or a decade later, and if they are lucky, 20, 30, 40 or 50 years on, will be different. This universal commonality I'm referring to should be clearly understood, because as time passes, people's desires, reactions, and expectations change. Making sure that all parties in the relationship are aware of these changes can be challenging, because the time of "what once was", most likely will not return, especially the longer you are together.

CHAPTER 4—IT'S BEST TO WAIT TO HAVE SEX UNTIL YOU'RE MARRIED

Jokingly in society, we often hear about a couple who have been together for "ages". The man in this situation is typically depicted as regularly denied sex from his wife due to her unwillingness or disinterest. And on the other side, the man has come home from work and at the end of the night before bed, instead of being ready for sex, is fast asleep before the lights are even turned off! All of these things, although assumed comical, in some degrees are quite often more a reality in many people's lives and all jokes aside, can lead to very unfulfilling relationships, leaving either partner or both of them feeling undesired and disconnected.

The misconception and eventual downfall in most of these situations is not tempering the realities of what extended time and age do to your sex life. In most cases, that change is a decrease or shift in the desire for as much sex, versus when you first met. As much as you or your partner may enjoy sex, there are many other features in a relationship that need to established, and it's rare to maintain the same high degree of sex. For many, if this isn't accepted as natural, it can be interpreted as a negative reflection on them, when in most cases, it's simply the next phase of a maturing relationship. In these moments, instead of blaming one another, it's crucial that you explore other parts of the relationship and help each other grow. The point is not to deny sex. On the contrary, the goal is to embrace the trajectory of change and encompass the new feelings and desires, while still enabling sex to integrate into the fold. It's not an easy shift and will take some getting used to, nonetheless accepting change versus holding on or fighting it in the long run will help your relationship embrace what should be considered normal and not fleeting or decaying.

SEXY CLOSEOUT

The chronicles of life and the emphasis that sex has had on people and in relationships has been one of the main focal points in the human narrative. The trouble remains, that as much time as we have had to evolve, it appears that we have not shifted much regarding raw acts and basic desires. This has left little room for imagination and even less emphasis on the deeper emotional, mental, and spiritual roles that sex reveals. This has led to a perverse understanding of sex and an inability to connect due to the unrealistic expectations and contaminated social norms that continue to plague modern society. On the other side, the naïve and romanticized way that sex has also been portrayed gives a false sense of reality, especially when the unexpected "prince" shows chinks in the armor and the "princess" has to learn about birth control.

That is why, for me personally, the topic of this chapter opens up uncomfortable and unknown situations that we are often faced with regarding sex. The fact that sex is also such an intimate and personal subject requires a more in depth and altruistic approach. When it's all said and done, sex remains a very instinctual behavior and we all have very specific wants, needs, and things we really don't have interest in.

But moving past the actual act of sex is when the real challenges awaken. Most people understand that although sex can be highly gratifying and fulfilling in the moment, the true desire to be able to grow and maintain a relationship far exceeds any sexual act. Even people who wait to have sex until after they are married are confronted with issues and require more than an instinct to get them through.

Achieving balance in sex and being able to evolve through the changes is a big part of life and a key to finding what makes a relationship work and what makes you happy.

CHAPTER 5

BLOOD IS THICKER THAN WATER
(Except when your rich father dies)

*"If you are betrayed, release disappointment at once.
By that way, the bitterness has no time to take root."*
—TOBA BETA

The stigmas and stereotypes around the family dynamic go back in history as long as we can remember. From the "crazy" aunt, the "rich" uncle, the "fun" dad to the "overprotective" mother, we can all relate to some degree to the diverse nature of family. In fact, we may be that very person with a stereotypical role or label in the family. Whatever character you play often comes at a cost. At times it's perceived as harmless or justified as "part of how the family is" or it may be so "normal" we have a limited perspective on what a healthy functioning family truly is.

My life came to another crashing halt when my map of how I understood family failed me, resulting from several unforeseen health issues with my father, that eventually led to his passing, and the actions and in some cases, lack of actions, my family prescribed during and after the event.

I knew that the world could be callous and cutthroat, but I had no idea it could come in the form of my own flesh and blood. In the past, I could recall many "incidents" of selfish and thoughtless acts performed by my family, but when those actions affected me personally, it was much more of a shock, and I questioned my standard of "accepting". This questioning ultimately led to my decision to separate from my family completely and realize there was nothing more to gain from maintaining what I had come to know as "How we had always been".

Dad was sick and had yet to be diagnosed with early onset Alzheimer's and dementia. The issue was that I lived in another state where I grew my business. The family and "people around him" were more worried about his assets and where his money was going when he died, versus getting a clear diagnosis of his illness. For over a year, I did all I could to recommend that dad get checked for what I believed to be failing memory and recall issues, but my pleas were continuously ignored or stalled. At one point, I was even given the absurd rationale that his hip was the issue and his mind was just fine! After hip surgery (seriously), his ability to remember continued to decline and simple task like using a remote control and phone became challenging. All the while, there was still no aggressive attempt made to address what had now become a clear indicator that his mental health was in jeopardy.

In my last attempt to outline a plan of action, I was told by a family member (let's call him Cain) that my actions were being perceived as trying to take over my dad's assets! For me that was the last straw. I would no longer focus my energy on something that was clearly going to be an uphill battle. Cain dug his claws in and he was truly unaware that the love for my father was more important than his money. The entire time the rest of the family urged me to fight him and justified that with me being the eldest son, I needed to "take control" of the family and set things right. I considered it, but my heart guided me to the conclusion that my father's peace of mind in his time of serious illness and decline in health, was more important. All I wanted was my dad's health back and fighting for his money seemed feeble. So, I walked away from it all and built my business, and during that time I sold my first company, liberating myself from financial struggle and burden. I didn't know that the worst lessons from my family were yet to be revealed.

For almost five years I heard very little from my family. Only on occasion would I get pictures of my father, and his total decline into Alzheimer's was now finally acknowledged and obvious in the pictures. I received word that his assets were being sold and his money being used to buy houses which was Cain's "business" and that he had not worked in years, all the while living off my dad's hard-earned money. As my dad's health continued to steadily decline, the news I received next shocked me the most. For the past couple of years my father had been in an assisted living community in Mexico with no family members closer than a state away. If the news about his money and assets was not enough to infuriate me, this news made my blood boil. I quickly retained an attorney and private investigator who both concluded foul play and that my father's assets should be frozen until there was a clear picture of Cain's intentions. For me it was not necessary, and no amount of fighting could ever bring the father I loved back. For me it was clear what the next step was, I had to see my dad for the last time. I needed to say goodbye.

After tracking him down, me and my mother made the trip to

Mexico. It was a desolate town and my father's accommodation was far beneath the standard that he was entitled to if his money was allocated appropriately and in his best interests. To my dismay, Cain had the audacity to "conveniently" be there at the same time we arrived. Fortunately for him, my mother was there whilst he slithered around with his "message of joy" about seeing us, talking as if we had been in touch and somehow connected, but in reality, we had not spoken in over five years. If my mother had not been present, I fear that both our fates would have changed and my life derailed, for the urge to "pay back" what he had done to us was strong.

    Focusing on my father, I walked to see him and as I entered the room, I was able to pick him out instantly. I hurried to embrace one of my best friends, my greatest teacher and my father. As I approached and he saw me, his eyes lit up and the first thing he said was "wow". I smiled and bent down to embrace him in the wheelchair to which he was now confined. I kissed his head and his scent immediately brought me back to his entirety and of the father I had always known.

    With his limited movement, he grabbed what was closest to his hands, which happened to be my head, and he squeezed it, hard. He squeezed it with such intensity, and I knew it was not out of anger, but out of the strength that was left in him to let me know just how much he loved me. At that moment all was well and as Cain continued talking with my mother, I embraced what would be the last afternoon I would ever spend with my father. I fed him lunch, which was now strictly a liquid diet (since he could not remember how to chew anymore) and when my mom approached him, he again said "wow". She embraced him and for the final afternoon hours we sat next to my father and although he couldn't form a complete sentence, I asked him questions and based on his response, we found peace in the moment. My mother and I said our goodbyes and my father passed on Christmas Day, the following year, 2021. Only once after his death did I hear from Cain. That was not a surprise, but what awaited me afterwards is what tipped the scales and commanded that I write this specific chapter in this book.

My dad had passed; he was at peace now and could rest. No amount of money mattered to me, but Cain sent me my inheritance with a note that would make anyone cringe. He stated, "We were all suffering because of our father's passing", and more phony nonsense and a drama-soaked script that made me laugh and wince all at once. I viewed the note as another sign to acknowledge just how deranged my family was and immediately sent the letter and inheritance back, telling Cain that I hope he "lives forever". My intent, was to clearly show the irony of the money being sent back as a moot point, and that my intentions had always gone far beyond my father's wealth.

I never received a call, letter, text, or any kind of support from my father's immediate family. This included my grandmother, uncle, aunt, and all of my cousins. To this day, I have heard nothing from them, and these non-actions enabled me to be free. Sadly, it was not much of a shock but more of a reality check; hoping for more, but not expecting it, and all the while providing me with all I would ever need to accept, forgive, and move on. But at the same time, shattering the age-old belief that "blood is thicker than water" and why I hope you understand the justification for the title of this chapter.

So, you've heard my story, now it's time to see if it may be the right moment for you to forgive and move on, or if there may be some more tread on the tires, to learn to forgive and grow the best way you can. Regardless, the goal of this chapter is not to hold a grudge or point fingers, the goal is to open your eyes to what you're feeling and help you navigate the toxic storms of some families. Obviously, I could not weather that storm and have since found peace and solitude with the only remaining relationship with my mother and no contact at all with my family, but that was after many years of hard situations, forgiveness, and acceptance. So, what do you do if you're facing a family crisis, and you fear that saying something will break the façade?

HERE ARE MY THOUGHTS:
The first step is to analyze the situation and determine if what is going on is toxic. In my example, it was pretty clear my father was being taken advantage of and that my family had very little interest in my well-being during his illness and after his death.

Here are some examples to give you an outside perspective, that many times helps us see what we have gotten so used to.

- Are the actions being taken by your family, loving and kind, and based on facts that do not alienate or divide the family members?

In my situation, it was clear that my father was being influenced by Cain for selfish reasons and when I questioned the "facts", instead of hearing me out, I was blamed. The rest of my family desired that I "take over" the situation, which gave no room for a civil exchange. In the end, it divided us, versus a fact-based scenario, which could have provided my dad with the best outcome. It's important to realize that even if you feel "your way" to help a family member appears to be the most loving, kind, and effective, it cannot be forced, only offered. At that point, it is up to the family to decide and up to you to accept their decision. Of course, you have the right to choose how you want to handle the situation, especially if you deem that the other person's decision has a harmful or negative impact.

- Is your family stuck in the "This is how it's always been" mentality?

This is one of the most common examples and can lead us to many unhealthy habits, also known as "the elephant in the room". Examples like: your dad has always been a drinker, your aunt has never taken her health seriously, or your brother deserved that since he didn't listen, are just a few illustrations that often have us turn a blind eye, thus enabling the patterns of our family to repeat. For me, a lack of compassion was a staple in my family. If you did not "fall in line" then you would be ostracized and eventually turned on. It wasn't until my dad's situation that I realized I was no different and met the same fate as all of my other family members in the past.

- Is a family that is toxic and familiar, better than healthy and questioning?

This is a touchy one, because families may have an 85-year-old grandfather who has religiously had his black coffee with a small shot of "goodness"; donuts, and a cigarette every weekend, and no one will dare challenge him to change. (That was like my Uncle Ernie, who for most his life and after serving in World War II, smoked like a train until weeks before his death in his 80s. You'll meet him later). And in those situations, you are hard pressed to implement change without it being a self-righteous act. It's okay to be kind and suggestive for a time, but if Grandpa wants to drink his spiked coffee, eat his donuts and smoke his cigarettes, then you should probably let him. However, it's when Grandpa wants to smoke near the children, or push some "goodness" on others, that it becomes an issue. It's when the unhealthy actions are imposed on others that you need to question the situation and speak up. At times this can cause a stir or a division, but if Grandpa can't understand that second hand smoking can cause major health issues, then it's your responsibility for yourself and the children to do what is best, even if that means walking away.

For me, that moment was after I received no word, or support from my family, after my father's death. I realized they would always be this way and instead of expecting them to change, and to find my peace and forgiveness, I needed to let go and be at peace with my actions. Otherwise, I would be stuck in the cycle that had consumed my family for generations.

- Does your family keep secrets and spread "news" about each other?

Another prickly subject is that of secrets and rumors. Both of these issues ran deep in my family. For as long as I can remember, it was not uncommon to "hear" about one of my uncle's sexual scenarios or mistresses and the issues it was causing with his immediate family, but that I should "keep it to myself". If it was true, it was of course troubling, but in my eyes, what made it worse, was how the family could be so careless and thoughtless about spreading this type of "news" about each other and not realize the effects it would have on a young boy. I recall our family gatherings and my perspective on my uncle and his family after being told of his affairs. Now I can never be certain, but I'm convinced most of the family knew what was going on and I could feel and see the tension from my uncle and the shame and embarrassment from his wife. The strangest part was that all the while, the rest of the family gloated over the fact that this information had been revealed. It was as if they could only view him and his wife based on these "secrets". Watching everyone's eyes and movements to see if any "deeper" or more dramatic reactions would occur, because of what they all "knew" based on the rumors. Looking back at this, it seems very strange, and I understand why my father did his best to distance himself from the family during his life and it's no surprise that I completely broke away.

However, the tie to our family may be very strong. Situations like the one I just shared are complex and at a young age, they could seem quite normal. The key is to look at the entire situation and ask yourself if you wish to keep any "secret", or spread any rumor. In the end, you can only control your part and that's all that matters. So, if it means you stop enabling the secrets and rumors, that's a great first step. The secrets and rumors will persist, but it's your choice if you engage in the toxic web.

For me, it was clear that it led to nothing but uncomfortable situations and toxic environments that were based on facades and power struggles. In my mind, that is not the way of a healthy and loving family.

FINDING THE BEST SOLUTION FOR YOUR LIFE
Family dynamics are never simple and no matter how big or small of

an influence you play, as long as you're involved, there will always be challenges to navigate. Nonetheless, there is never a bad time to heal, grow, and strengthen your relationships in your family. Assuming there is growth potential and a reciprocal approach, doing so with no blinders on and the acceptance that all parties can see the issues that need to be changed, it is a great opportunity.

Like in my situation, some things may feel beyond your energy and desire to repair and it's better to limit your time and engagement, especially with the family members that you feel just don't have the desire to transform. For many (including myself) the "responsibility" that was bestowed upon me was great and it took many years to realize that the best solution for my life was not to feel guilty about issues that were toxic or uncomfortable. This meant drawing boundaries and making them known, which in turn led to much disdain, anger and resentment from my family, that in turn helped me realize I needed to walk away. This may not be the best situation for everyone and hopefully your family situation is not as fractured and beyond repair as mine.

Before my dad's illness, I held my family in high regard and esteem and even through all the obvious toxic traits and behavior, there was always a great sense of love and pride we all shared. After my dad became ill, the foundation was shaken and never the same. Everyone became less involved, and many never resurfaced. For some, blood may indeed be thicker than water, but when your rich father dies, you see who really has the strength to do what is right for the family as a whole, and not only for themselves. Be aware of what can and should be done for a healthy and loving familial relationship, and always make sure it matches your morals and beliefs, and never sacrifice them for anyone, family included.

CHAPTER 6

COMPASSION AND FORGIVENESS
MAKE YOU A GOOD PERSON
(Except when you have an agenda)

*"Compassion is to look beyond your own pain,
to see the pain of others."*
—YASMIN MOGAHED

A great man once said, "Let him who is without sin, cast the first stone." Wise words to live by and no higher moral obligations to emulate. Compassion and forgiveness are some of the most critical tools to have in life and can help take the "I" and "me" out of tough situations, and support the bridge of challenging gaps we often encounter. Like all moral choices, how we go about both compassion and forgiveness is important to maximize and ensure our actions are authentic. This is very crucial if you want to truly find closure and peace and be able to move on with your life.

It's not uncommon we forgive because we are told we "should" or because it's "the right thing to do", but internally we still may harbor feelings of anger, animosity, pain or guilt. We are also told to have compassion for people, but if that person has hurt you, or someone or something you love or cherish, it makes having compassion much more challenging and at times feels impossible.

In this chapter, I want to guide you through some steps and share insights on how to reach genuine compassion and forgiveness and to be able to identify if you are on the right path. I will lay out some "to dos" and maybe more importantly some, "what not to dos", which helped me out just as much or more. But before we jump into the specifics, I'll share a personal story on why compassion and forgiveness helped me heal and grow in ways I never thought possible.

In the past, there were many times in my life that I forgave, but depending on the "severity" of the situation, the forgiveness came with stipulations. For instance, if someone betrayed me, in my mind I felt they should eventually be forgiven, but were never to be trusted again. Whereas, if something less severe took place, I would forgive them, but make sure I kept close tabs and a "score". I would then use those instances to remind them of past infractions, and to justify why I would not fully commit, convincing myself it was for my protection. I continued this process for years and although there was some relief and closure, deep inside, unfulfilled responsibility weighed me down. As much as I could feel the pull to do more in the realm of forgiveness, it wasn't until I sought to be forgiven, that I realized how authentic forgiveness, without a catch or agenda, changed my life and freed my soul.

As I mentioned early in the book, the poor decisions I made regarding my past relationship eventually made it impossible for us to continue. If that wasn't enough, this person I loved felt so wounded and betrayed by my actions, she could not find the ability to truly forgive me. The irony being it was a mirror image of how I treated others in similar situations. It was not until I realized how much I desired forgiveness and the daunting possibility that I would never receive it, did it truly sink in.

Over two years passed, and I suffered heavily with guilt, shame, and remorse. I yearned for the opportunity to redeem myself, but knew redemption would only come when the other person was willing to hear me out with an open heart. It finally occurred to me that waiting for forgiveness from another person was not effective if I wanted to find peace. So, I decided to forgive myself. But where could I begin? Initially, I fought with the idea and wrestled with the guilt in my mind, that constantly seemed to have only one goal, which was to prevent me from forgiving myself. But as time passed, I slowly took the steps to build a new map. Once I identified and committed to a regimen, I saw a light at the end of the tunnel. I made the decision that I would find forgiveness and peace, with or without another person. As I worked through the last stages of grief, guilt and pain, a remarkable thing happened.

After over two and a half years, I received an email from my former partner, not only forgiving me, but also thanking me for what we shared during all those years together. Tears of joy flowed down my face, and the weight that was lifted was almost indescribable. What I wanted for all that time had finally happened and it was not only more than I could have imaged, but it provided me with something much deeper. I had been given a gift, and I realized that if this was how I felt when someone forgave me, then moving forward, I would forgive with the fullness of my heart and without an agenda. This lesson forever changed me and my life, and the way it transpired could not have been more perfect. As usual, the universe provided, and I was fortunate enough to have an open heart and mind to understand what I had received.

I admit this situation is rare and for many people it doesn't work out in this manner. If it does, consider yourself fortunate. If it doesn't, here are some of those steps I mentioned to help you find forgiveness and resolution.

FORGIVE WITH NO STRINGS ATTACHED

By far, one of the most challenging requirements of achieving authentic compassion and forgiveness is being able to let go completely once you have forgiven. A true test of this will be revealed after you answer the following questions:

- Would you be at peace knowing that you could never talk or reconcile with a person who hurt or betrayed you, or who you hurt or betrayed?

- Would you want peace for a person after they hurt or betrayed you?

- Would you be able to not "keep score" from a previous betrayal and look at each new moment without residual disdain, anger, or judgment?

- Would you be able to have little to no response when a past betrayal or painful experience is sparked? (Not because you are ignoring it or pushing it away, but because you have processed it fully and can be accountable for your role in the exchange.)
- Would you be able to put yourself in the other person's situation versus defending yours, to help better understand

"why" from their perspective, instead of remaining the "victim"?

- Would you be able to accept that painful actions and betrayals do not justify a closed heart for future relationships and that it's your choice to trust again?

- Would you be able to accept that only through the lens of love and compassion can you forgive and find true peace, and that no actions, no matter how vile, can ever justify your inability to forgive?

- Would you be able to accept that it's your choice to remain angry, scared, resentful and the victim, if hurt or betrayed, and that the reality is that your feelings stem from your choices and that no one can "make you feel this way"?

- Would it be simpler to let go of pain, anger, and resentment, or is holding on easier?

If you answered no to any of the following, then obviously there is work to be done in the form of reflecting. Part of processing the desire to forgive is to be gentle with yourself and to realize that it does not excuse the actions that caused the pain. The point is not about the other person, it's about what forgiveness does for you. If your goal is truly to forgive, you should be prepared and understand that the path towards this goal will come with its challenges, but ultimately, the transformation will change your life. That was the case for me.

> *"I think part of the reason why we hold on to something so tight is because we fear something so great won't happen twice."*
> —UNKNOWN

- Do not romanticize the past. Do not discount it either.

The past can be a tricky thing and can bare our greatest wounds, as well as our most precious memories. If not handled correctly, dwelling on either makes little room for the present and can keep us in a fog. The past has great value and provides experiences for us to learn and grow. But like all things, being truthful about what is, versus what was or could have been, is a skill that takes constant effort to develop. Far too often we let the "good old days" creep into our thoughts, comparing how great things "used to be", or worse yet, let unresolved fears and pain stunt our ability to advance. The saying "once bitten, twice shy", is an appropriate reminder of when we let our past dictate our present and our future.

I know the temptation from first-hand experience and I can tell you it almost buried me. The weight of holding on to the past was almost unmanageable and before long, almost two years had gone by. I reminisced about how great things were and got stuck on what I "could have done better". This cycle of thought is natural and healthy, but unfortunately, I became obsessive and allowed the past to overshadow my life and my ability to move forward. After continued work (which I will outline) I came to realize that the only situation I could change **was my thoughts of the current moment**. A simple statement, but one that requires a vast amount of effort, focus, and commitment. This is how I got there.

- Don't jump into another relationship

You would assume that this goes without saying... But the fact that it is the first one on the list is no coincidence. No matter what "side" you feel you were on, you still played a role in the undoing of your relationship. To be naïve, or worse, arrogant enough to put all the blame on the other person, is a major oversight. Then, to think you can jump right back into a relationship with someone else without doing any work, will more often than not, lead you back to the same path. Only after you know who you are by the mistakes you have made; can you hope to be better at making healthier decisions. This is why being alone and finding refuge in your thoughts and habits is necessary. Using time to reflect on oneself, supports and purifies our internal guidance and magnifies what we may have always known to be true, but previously had a difficult time understanding or utilizing. A good example for me was having the bad habit of trying to save the person I was with. After I gave myself this alone time to reflect, I realized the depths of my habits and in response, have now found it much easier to walk away from overly dependent people and stop being the enabler. If I had jumped back into another relationship, I don't think I would have seen this pattern and would have been destined to repeat it.

- Healthy diet, exercise, rest and no drugs or alcohol.

The foundation of our abilities is tied to the fact we are flesh and blood. When your mind and emotions are fighting to find their equilibrium, your most basic needs should always be addressed first. Keeping your body as healthy as possible supports a clear mind, which allows optimal decision making and improved outcomes. It baffles me when people drink their pain away or think getting high will magically change anything. On the contrary, it only numbs you, makes you more depressed when you come down from the high and realize you are in the exact same situation you were prior. When facing a difficult past, we must be fully prepared to do whatever necessary, and a sound mind and body make it easier to accomplish.

- Read. A lot.

There is no easy path to finally let go of the past and embrace the moment. Many times, we feel that if we let go of what was, it somehow makes the good memories less sacred. Or if we hold on to the bad memories, it can help justify our fears, pain, and anger. Nothing could be further from the truth. Yet day-to-day life often fails to provide answers and just trying to survive becomes a task within itself. This is why reading is so crucial in the process and can help identify concepts that could potentially be the key to your understanding and salvation. Personally, I read everything on relevant topics that I could get my hands on. I went to Amazon and searched for books on forgiveness, letting go, codependency, or whatever I felt would help me heal and I bought at least five books on each topic. I did this for many years and although there was much overlap and redundancy, the habitual lessons soaked into my consciousness, and helped me to overcome my inability to stop romanticizing the past. To this day and for the rest of my life, I will read insightful books, knowing that each page helps me fill in my "map", which enables me to grow in times of hardship. The gifts a masterful book can provide are priceless and well worth the effort even if only one "gem" is uncovered.

- Journal every day (data dump) or write a book

This exercise took me some time to adapt, but once I did, I could mentally feel the release. It's been observed that if you write your thoughts out consistently, it opens up your ability to think more clearly and discharge what you accumulate. The most intriguing part I witnessed was how I wrote would change based on the emotions I felt at the time of journaling. For example, if I was calm and stable, my penmanship would reflect the same. However, if I was sad or angry, the contrast was unmistakable and dramatic. Writing just a sentence or even a few words was not uncommon when I was heated. Over time, I saw the results and wanted to take it a step further, thus the idea for this book was born. Writing a book is not for everyone, but if you have the will and the desire, the growth and reflection can change your life. It did for me.

- Go to therapy

Talking to a professional is always a wise option if your self-guided attempts fail, or if you need an alternative vantage point. A therapist's job is not to tell you what to do, but to help you reflect on what you may not be able to see or understand. Although it's great to speak with trusted family and friends, many times they hold a biased perspective that reinforces, versus makes you reflect or be accountable to change. This is why speaking with a therapist offers a neutral perspective, which you need to release how you view the past and what role you played.

- Embrace God or spiritually

For those of us who have a form of God or spiritually in our lives, typically the best time to utilize faith is when we have the inability to change things or can't find the answers to our deepest questions. The fact that the past can never be revisited or changed makes this one of life's biggest challenges and why so many people get stuck. Although each faith is different, in most cases, there is great relief when you can turn to your God or spiritual practice to guide you to clarity. In life, there will be many unanswered questions, and God or spirituality can be one of the best remedies to find peace of mind.

- Realizing you have an agenda and learning how to let it go

It's rare that we correlate having an agenda to a bad habit. Having an agenda for things such as goals, can be a positive thought system, but regarding forgiveness, it can be a major crutch. To learn something new takes time and commitment. Arguably, to unlearn something takes just as much commitment, or even more. When we think of "bad habits" our thoughts turn to common addictions such as overindulging in alcohol, drugs, food, and working too much. This is why people often fall into the trap of being unaware of what true forgiveness means and continuously fall short.

So, what is "true forgiveness"? As I mentioned earlier, letting go with no strings attached and not having expectations is a great start. But for each person, the details differ and because of that, we may try to justify our "unique" situation, making it hard to let go completely. At the end of the day, forgiveness has no rank order. There is no "worse" situation that justifies any agenda. For many, that is the rub that makes it very difficult to acknowledge. People don't want to hear that if someone murders or rapes, versus cheating or drunk driving, that the same rules of forgiveness apply. To acknowledge and accept this, means to give away our defense and rationale to hold on to blame. From the outside, it makes sense that murder or rape justify greater anger, and only to forgive after justice is served. But even so, the truth remains inside. It is only when we let go with authentic peace and resolve that the true benefits of forgiveness without an agenda can take place.

- Now that you have done the work, true compassion and forgiveness can start.

The examples I have provided are what helped me, and if implemented and practiced diligently, I assure you they will help establish a more authentic outlook on true compassion and forgiveness. Of course, these are not the only methods available, but are a great starting point to help you branch out to what works best for you.

I cannot understate the need to "do the work" and "practice diligently", as what got us into many undesirable situations takes a ton of intentional, consistent, and often painful effort. Being accountable and reflecting on one's shortcomings is never easy. However, if the pain of what you experienced was greater than your desire to repeat it, there is no alternative for liberation. That is why having a clear framework for after your "map" has run out is key. And like many bad habits, it takes a serious decision to be committed to embrace change and see it through. There are rewards and true light at the end of the tunnel.

CHAPTER 7

YOU DESERVE RESPECT
(Except when you don't care what anyone thinks)

*"Those who await respect rarely deserve it,
those who command respect need not ask."*
—UNKNOWN

I have studied people who are well respected and often come to the same conclusion. They do what they need to do, regardless of how they are perceived, and they take complete accountability for their actions. If you only take action based on how others view you versus what you know to be true, you cannot be truly authentic. This is especially the case for situations that initially may cost you to "lose" or let something go. It's one thing to stand behind black and white decisions, but another when we deal in a grey life and world.

For many, being respected is a sign and acknowledgment of status and accomplishment. Why does respect matter? More importantly, I think, we should ask, why doesn't it matter? Growing up, respect was a big part of my life. Culturally speaking it began early, with the Mexican side of my family being very proud and the men especially what we called "machismo". As I grew up around this mindset, I took it as a badge of honor and made it a point to always ensure I was respected. At times this meant being very aggressive and even getting into fights when I felt disrespected. As life continued and I entered sports (martial arts and basketball) the level of respect required and often demanded, grew as the competition increased. The "bigger and badder" you wanted to become, the fiercer the respect needed to be. Like for most young men, the hierarchy of this environment had its pecking order and the only way to level up, was to impose your will and instill respect in your opponents. Even your teammates needed to gain your respect and until the hierarchy was established, I often found myself fighting with them.

As I grew out of sports and into adulthood, my career mentality encompassed what I had learned from my family and as an athlete. However, the outcomes weren't as fluid, and I often ran into walls, leaving all parties frustrated and even offended. Imposing my will was a tactic that had worked very well in the past, and my assumption was it would be the same in other areas of life. I quickly realized that sheer force and intimidation was a limited tool in business and could actually be more detrimental in some cases. Respect was not measured by how many fights you won, or points you scored, but by so much more. It took me many years to figure out how to balance my super intense approach with the almost unspoken "rules" of business. Because in reality, most great athletes are not great businesspeople and most great businesspeople are not great athletes.

As time passed, I learned to temper my built-in response as an athlete, with the reality that I was now playing in the business world with different rules. I had to lose my fixation that respect was the most important thing, regardless of the situation and once I did, a major part of my life completely changed.

The change didn't happen overnight, and in fact, in many situations I was unable to hold my tongue and I paid for it. It took many years to humble myself and live by the mantra "I would rather win, than be right" and although I have become good at it, even to this day, if pushed enough, it's challenging for me not to overreact. If you take a minute to think about that quote, you too may reflect on situations where you were more focused on being right and instilling your point, then you were on winning. Afterwards we feel ashamed of creating an uncomfortable situation that did not help either party, and although you may have got your point across and feel justified and "right", you leave the situation no better than you found it and, in many times, much worse.

Personally, I'm the type that needs real life experience to truly understand. I wish this was not the case and that I could take someone's word for it, read a book, or watch a video to help convince me that how it was explained, was accurate. But sadly, this is not how I process and because of that I have to learn the hard way. My desire is to share some tools and processes that bypass the hard knocks and help keep your ego in check.

RULE 1—*If you know something well enough (mastery) you should be able explain it in under 60 seconds*
The first thing that comes to mind for many on this rule is the "elevator pitch". Basically, you have one minute to sell yourself. No simple task and even more challenging if you are new to your career. How does this relate to respect? Well, the more you master anything, the faster you can explain it. Furthermore, any questions, disputes, or challenges can

be resolved with ease. Again, you may ask, how does respect tie into this? I'm getting there, I promise. They say knowledge is power and no matter how old the cliché, it never disappoints. For many (myself included) power was tied to respect, but respect needs to be earned and only through mastery is true respect achieved. It is rare to find someone who masters anything in life, but the few that take that approach rarely seem to worry about being respected. Their bodies of work speak for themselves and if they are challenged, it has little impact on what they have already achieved. It's not to say that any dispute of mastery is not worthy of consideration, but mastery has overcome so many potential rebuttals that it takes a very special person to challenge it. A master has no time to care about what anyone thinks because they are too consumed with how to achieve what they have set out to do. This path, almost by default, commands not caring about anything but the goal, so whether they are respected or not is of no consequence to the person who truly embodies what they have set out to do.

If you ever take the time to watch a master at work, you will see that they have little room for anything else. A great example is when an athlete gets in "the zone" or when a musician loses themselves in the song, they are singing or the instrument they are playing. What appears to be second nature for them has taken tens of thousands of hours to accomplish. Through that refinement is where simplicity emerges and what can then be explained quite effortlessly. Many great artists or musicians claim they can "just see" or "just hear" the piece before it's been accomplished or composed and although talent and timing have a role in each situation, a vast majority of those "special abilities" come from an almost obsessive commitment to the craft or goal. Basically, when a person decides they want to become masterful at something, it's my understanding that the need for respect leaves the equation. It has no place in a process that requires humility, patience, and setbacks. Letting go of the need for respect opens up more space and gives the individual the most fluidity on the path towards mastery.

RULE 2—*Recognize that most people are in the stands and not in the game.*
Having compassion and understanding, while at the same time taking care of oneself, is a balance in life that will always have its challenges. It's rare that any path we take is completely desolate and without the opinions of others. Yet, what's important is how much we allow feedback to affect us.

For the most part, each person's "insight" is personal and relative to their own experiences and viewpoints. Although it's always wise to listen, the first few questions you should consider before investing too much time in others' thoughts are the following:

- Are they successful in the topic or action being discussed? Meaning top of their respected field or industry and have always put integrity and truth at the top of their agendas while conducting themselves.

- How close are you? How long have you known them? Several years, several months, or have you just met?

- Have they historically had your best interests in mind? The selfless and caring, without judgment, typically give advice only when asked, or give you a heads up when you may be running into potential problems they know about.

- Do they have an agenda for giving you this information or feedback? Is it honest or are there ulterior motives?

For me, the first question dictates everything else and could be all you need to ask yourself. If you want basketball advice, watching or listening to Michael Jordan is better than listening to your uncle who played in high school. If you want relationship advice from your dad who has been divorced three times, it may not be the best idea to emulate him on what love and marriage "should look like".

Unfortunately, we all have to deal with friends or family that are quick to provide their insight, but fail to recognize that their track records, and no matter how good their intentions, are not the most potent and effective forms of counsel. This is frequently uncovered when we approach something with little experience, or only the influence of these individuals. This leads to learning the hard way and may become another statistic or failed attempt. The hope is that as we evolve, we focus on absorbing the best of what each person has to offer.

The intention behind a person's mastery or success is also an important aspect to analyze and consider. How a person builds mastery is just as important as what has been mastered. Far too often as a society, we look at great levels of success, mastery, and achievement with tunnel vision and an all-out blanket approach. Enabling a "they can do no wrong" mentality and thinking that the one thing this person mastered gives them authority over a larger scope of issues then truly reasonable.

It has also become common practice to perpetuate a victim

mentality, to justify crude and reckless behavior for the sake of "coming up" or reaching success. But as much as we feel we can separate intentions from actions, it becomes much clearer as you embark on your own path to mastery and realize that selflessness and truthful intentions will give you a much deeper and lasting fulfillment. It's one thing to emulate a habit, pattern, or approach that gives you a higher degree for the chance of succeeding (an example could be, proper form in a sport, or the best time to send out an email) but the "secret sauce" comes from one's intentions, which in my experience always provides that extra magic.

Historically, exceptional humans who mastered something identified a deeper purpose. It's crucial to understand your purpose because it makes it much clearer for you to realize if your intentions match up, or if you have to adjust your parameters. For example, those who came from little means and have "nothing to lose", would be hard pressed to relate or identify with someone who came from a well-to-do environment. But this is one of the biggest mistakes we overlook and why it often leads to failure in our attempts at mastery. Of course, we are all built differently and think differently, but there are obvious similarities that need to be considered while you are analyzing intentions.

UP TO HERE

The next piece to consider is who this person is to you. How long have you known them and how close are you? It seems fairly obvious that time builds stronger rapport and closer relationships, but it might surprise you how often people divulge too much, too quickly. Trust can take a lifetime to build and a moment to break and is why it's crucial to constantly analyze who you take advice from. It's necessary to be aware of what you say and when you say it. Far too much time is lost listening to people you don't know on a deeper level, and not only can you not get that time back, but you also leave yourself exposed to situations you might want to avoid. Now, this is not to say that you can't make impactful connections relatively quickly. In fact, the closer you get to mastery, the more the people around you become attracted to your intentions and mind frame. Even so, the energy at high levels moves fast and fluid, so if you are not completely clear on your position and intentions, then it's advisable that you say less and listen more.

As you continue the vetting process of the people in your life, consider if they can historically claim that they have had your best interests in mind. Selfless and caring, without judgment, typically giving advice only when asked, or giving you a heads up when you may be running into a potential problem they know about? If you can answer yes to all of these, then this person is someone you would be wise to keep close. Especially in the difficult times in your life when what you need to hear is more important than what you want to hear.

I'm fortunate to say that this person for me is my mother. Growing up and to this day, I have never had anyone look out for my best interests like her. This is not as easy as it sounds, because many times what she sees and points me toward can be a hard lesson, or a bad habit I have ignored. It's easy to praise and support when times are good, but to be selfless when what has to be said is a painful reality can cause friction. This is why I always go back and ask her the hard questions. Only a few times in my life has she come to me before I have asked. And in those times, I was headed down a road that would most likely lead to more pain and destruction if I wasn't warned.

If you're not fortunate to have a family member close to you, consider a friend that may have the ability to know you well enough to tell it like it is. The power behind being able to ask for guidance from a trusted person who has your best interests at heart is priceless. Being honest is not always easy, but it can save you so much time and prevent hard lessons you may subconsciously not know about.

If you don't have a family member or friend that you feel you can trust in this manner, then you should ask yourself what is preventing you from forming these kinds of relationships. It's understandable that trust takes time to build, however, having no source of faith or confidence in anyone is a deep-rooted reservation that will limit your ability to maximize yourself. In life, we need people and should embrace the abilities of others to love and care for us. It's one of the things that makes humans unique and can provide a plethora of rewards. You can always start small and slow, but with an open heart and the intent to trust and grow. Otherwise, if you go into a situation anticipating failure or deceit, it tends to lower your chances of success.

Assuming you have identified this individual that has your best interest in mind, the final piece becomes establishing whether they have an agenda. As I mentioned earlier, there can be an endless supply of feedback from people, and most people love to tell you how they think something "should be". The problem with that is, most people are drastically underqualified. The good news is that today it's much easier to find a highly qualified person, a master or professional in any situation. The internet provides an endless supply of resources, and you can supplement feedback with more specific information. However, there are also a ton of deep and personal situations that no amount of internet resources can solve and that only a close family member or friend can help you through. Be aware of what solution fits best for the desired outcome and insight needed.

RULE 3—*Be able to laugh at yourself... A lot...*
Humility is an important lesson to learn in life and, if not recognized quickly, will often impose itself on you one way or another. Having a solid foundation through mastery can lighten your experiences, since you are able to take both bad and good situations as part of the journey, versus taking it personally. To be able to have fun, be lighthearted and laugh at yourself, shows a buoyant level of confidence and maturity, which helps aid in one's abilities to overcome many things. There is a big difference between taking yourself too seriously and what you do seriously. There is nothing wrong with having intense passion and focus. In fact, it's a key ingredient to mastery. But it can get confused and intertwined with the individual, who then holds a disposition of arrogance and entitlement, which gives off the "I deserve respect" vibe. Many people get stuck in this spot and, although they may have accomplished vast amounts, they fail in the humility category. The most dynamic people are those who do, without looking for praise. This shows the depth of one's character and empowers others by being open and humble. It's rare to come across these sorts of people, but when you do, it's almost undeniable that you can sense their greatness, even with nothing being said. This is by far the ultimate goal and why you don't need respect when you live with great purpose and mastery. It will come all on its own.

RULE 4—*Learn how to pass through a painful memory*
There is a fine line between what you try to express and what you need to understand. As long as what you are doing is not

intentionally harming others, or imposing your will without their clear understanding, then you can disregard anything and everything that is trying to slow you down, get in your way, or stop you. But it shouldn't end there. The next challenge should be doing it fast and forgetting all about it. This is where having a "painful memory" comes in handy. People hold resentment, anger, and guilt, and justify it as fuel. Although there is a debate on this subject, I tried this for many years, but there is a problem. After you get to your goal or have proved your point, you typically run out of the fuel that prompted the focus and must then redirect it. Predictably, it is done in the same manner, which is through resentment, animosity, or anger.

In my last book, *The Real Estate Bible,* there is a whole chapter that talks about clean fuel and why what you are using as motivation is important. Good fuel in, good fuel out, bad fuel in.... When you think about it, you lose all control when you let another person dictate your motivation. True strength must go deeper, true meaning should be self-reflecting or a helpful act for others. It should not be trying to "get one up", "told you so", or "going to get you back" mind frame. "Not caring" should mean you are confident and at peace with yourself, but far too often it's weaponized for aggression and retaliation. The energy lost that could be reallocated if directed with a "clean" approach is by far more sustainable for the long haul, and as you mature, you realize that.

RULE 5—*Love your haters*
This is a nice segue from Rule 4. Instead of being mad at your haters, embrace them. When people direct their time and energy for the sole purpose of attempting to break you, it can be a blessing in disguise. Of course, the mindless banter and hollow efforts with no facts or proof

should not apply. However, there can be significant benefits to a hater's critique, and it can be exactly what you couldn't see and what you need to improve. With that said, I recommend you don't focus on this. A good rule of thumb to investigate is if the SAME issues of hate and critique keep popping up. If there is a pattern, then they may be on to something. Otherwise, don't get lost in reacting or responding more than you need to, as it takes you away from your focus and goals. Life is all about perspective, so if you study everything introduced to you, both the bad and the good, it helps keeps things moving. So next time you get some hate, turn it into an advantage.

RULE 6—*Legacies are not necessary*
If you desire to live in truth, then having a legacy will never be your goal. In fact, building a legacy is one of the most egotistical based justifications. To claim a legacy is pompous, and only a ploy to label something that has recently been socially accepted as a "just cause", but is only enabling the ego's desires to be admired. Do you think Gandhi, Mother Teresa, MLK, Christ or Buddha embarked on building a legacy for themselves? Do you think that was their motivation and what propelled their historic accomplishments and notoriety? I would say absolutely not. And here lies our current problem, where the understanding and ideal of legacy has been perverted. To build anything that can be deemed a legacy, need not be self-defined. True legacies build themselves without the desire for it to be so. Humble yourself to your task and no other purpose, but the goals of truth shall matter. From there, everything is accomplished and forever infused with what a legacy is meant to embody.

Respect is one of the most powerful forms of providing a

compliment. It empowers people; it gives them confidence and the will to move through life. To embody respect in a form that is objective, just, consistent, and loving is a major advantage in life. If you can genuinely give respect, then you will receive it by default.

Great leaders can meet any person in any situation and look upon them with love and compassion. That is respect. The age old saying that you should treat a janitor the same way you treat a CEO, will always be true. Never demand respect, earn it. Never hold back respect, give it freely, unless shown why you should not. Respect may be the only thing two people meeting for one time in their lives can provide to each other. So, in that interaction, your sole responsibility could be to provide that. In doing so, with honor and integrity, you may be giving another person a huge lift and a small nudge in a better direction. Never avoid looking for a way to respect someone. I believe you should try to find as many reasons to respect them as you can. Give it a try and see how much better they feel, and what it does to lift your spirits.

CHAPTER 8

THE WORLD OWES YOU SOMETHING
(Except, it really doesn't)

*"When you come from a place of not needing anything,
or seeking anything outside yourself to make you happy,
you open up space for more amazing things to enter your life."*
—UNKNOWN

When I started college, like most young adults, I did not have much to call my own. My roommate and I pitched in for the living area of our small two-bedroom apartment and I bought my bedroom furniture from Goodwill. At six foot two, a full-sized bed was tight for me, and I wanted to save up enough money to buy a king size. I figured that if I bought the frame, my "well to do" dad would be more than willing to assist with the mattress. When the time came, I set it up, but had to use my full-sized mattress, in the middle of the giant frame. I assumed it would only be for a short time before my dad supplied the king size, and I could handle the inconvenience for a bit. What I did not expect was his response. Simply put, he refused and asked why I thought he should pay for it. At first, I was caught off guard. My rational mind figured a mattress was a necessity, and asking for help seemed reasonable enough. I tried to explain this to him, but to no avail. So, for the next four months, I was stuck sleeping on a full-size mattress, surrounded by a kind sized frame until I could afford to buy the new mattress.

From that day on, I realized that the only person I could ever rely on was me. I would like to think that at the time my dad had a deeper meaning and life lesson in his decision. However, when it was discussed later, it was clear he just didn't want to buy it. I'm not sure if I would have preferred him to lie to me, or if the cold truth of how the world can be served me better. Regardless, it was a life lesson that stuck with me and one I often recalled when I thought somebody owed me something.

In today's world, entitlement is less the exception and more a rule. This has led to people replacing gratitude with a self-indulgent pity party. In fact, it has gotten so bad, many expect the same response and services in almost all categories of life, even if they pay half the normal price. Even free has become somewhat expected or even "not good enough" if the standard doesn't meet their approval.

I don't believe it is ever okay to act entitled, but the point I want to make is that ordering a hamburger from a fast-food place, versus buying a new luxury car, enables certain degrees of expectations. If you get one pickle instead of two, or ketchup instead of mustard, you might be slightly annoyed. If you drive off the lot in your new car and the AC stops working, or a check engine light comes on, it makes sense to turn up the frustration meter a bit more. But this is not what I see happening. It's not uncommon nowadays to see people being belligerent and downright aggressive to a fast-food worker who forgot the pickle. Having no regard for the severity of the situation and being so self-centered and entitled, it would make a four-year-old cringe.

As a child, I was told you get more bees with honey than with vinegar, and it takes the same time to respectfully request that your issue be fixed as it does to be rude. This goes for the malfunctioning car situation as well, where people often think that because they purchased a bigger ticket item, it somehow permits them to treat the employees at the dealership like second-class citizens. I have seen both instances firsthand and both are inappropriate. This lack of respect has become a chronic problem and, in some ways, an almost accepted behavior in today's society. If you want people to listen to you, help you, or follow you, there is no room for entitlement. The quickest way to alienate yourself from others is to be entitled. Not only will you lose all respect, but don't be surprised when things get difficult and you require a helping hand, that you have little to no support. It can even go a step further where people will intentionally help sabotage you or look the other way, knowing you may be falling into a bad situation. All of this is because of entitlement.

There is, of course, a fine balance and nothing wrong with asking for what is fair if you feel short-changed. But when you ask, how you ask, and who you ask, all need to be considered, and that is where most people don't have a clue. I'll expand using the following rules:

RULE 1—*When to ask for something*
In a world of instant gratification, many have forgotten to have patience and respect, and act like spoiled children, instead of being grateful. Both examples (the fast food and new car) require a solution. When you're picking up "fast food" the whole purpose is expediting the process. So, when the system gets mucked up, it needs to be fixed

fast. The car situation may also require a rapid request to address the problem, but the overall remedy may not be as speedy.

So, let's use another example: your husband or wife just arrived home from a long day. You have been at home most of the day tidying the house. During your day, you have been thinking about "all the things" your partner "could do better to improve". Here are your options. Do you?

> A) Start sharing your thoughts within the first moments they get home.
> B) Wait until they have settled and discuss with them at dinner or after dinner.
> C) Ask about their day and see if it's a suitable time, or whether picking another time or even day would be more appropriate.
> D) Not care what their day was like and start talking to them about how they can improve, anyway.

The funny part is most people will pick everything except C and wonder why they don't get the most out of their ideas. Then blame the other person and feel as though they are the victim because they were not heard WHEN they wanted to be. Timing is an art and not really a science and often a very difficult act to perfect. But most people don't take it into consideration and prematurely react, which leads to a suboptimal exchange. The last thing you want to do is become the victim, when what you could have done was be more thoughtful.

Stepping back to look at the whole situation gives you a much better chance to decide if the timing is prime. It is not an easy thing to adjust to, but in the long run making a more conscious effort of WHEN to ask for something, typically produces a much more productive and harmonious listener, which then produces a better outcome for all.

RULE 2—*How to ask for something*
This seems pretty straightforward. Speak clearly, with respect, and listen when it's the other person's time to talk. But in current times, more people seem to blurt out an unthoughtful and incomplete reaction-based response, and if they don't get the reply they want, they raise their voice, and have little concern about what anyone else says.

My response is that, facts don't require excessive feelings.

If you are angry, sad, scared, tired, or emotional and the moment can wait, then it's best to hold off until you have composed yourself. Of course, life rarely allows ample time, so the next best thing is to be as calm and composed as you can and try to listen as much as possible. It's also wise to be open to any and all responses and not expect a certain answer (remember my mattress story!). This will help you cope, especially if you don't get the reply you anticipated.

Tone of voice, facial and physical expressions, are also crucial in HOW you ask for something. Looking someone in the eyes is a sign of confidence and assurance and bodes well for your request. If you avoid eye contact, it can give the impression that you lack resolve and authority.

Being animated is appropriate sometimes, but use caution, as too much movement can distract, or even intimidate, and reduce the impact of what you are trying to convey.

Thinking about who the person is, what their traits and habits are and even rehearsing HOW you are going to ask for something is also a great idea. It's not uncommon for me to rehearse in the mirror several times and anticipate different responses before speaking to someone. Being calm helps your speech be clearer and more fluid, which enables a more impactful and dynamic request.

Stepping back and thinking about HOW to ask for something can make a big difference in your life. It will encourage you to be more patient, selfless, and aware of not only what you want, but what others are feeling and want as well. There is nothing wrong with asking for what you want, but it doesn't mean you'll always get it. However, HOW you ask can always be done with class and respect for others and should be the standard regardless of whether you get a yes or no reply.

RULE 3—*Who to ask*

In life and work, there are many levels, and each level brings different requirements and scenarios. There are line employees, gatekeepers, managers, vice presidents, CEOs, founders, partners, and the list goes on. The point is, WHO to ask for something plays a major role in HOW and ironically WHEN you should ask. Hopefully, the tie in with the past two rules is clear. I will not go into what each position entails or what approach is most appropriate, as that should be part of your due diligence as you proceed. Common sense will tell you that your tactics for a CEO should differ from those when dealing with a line employee. Regardless, both should be treated with respect while being addressed appropriately for their positions. The CEO for his or her commitment to getting to the top of their company and the line employee for the skill and work that helps make the enterprise function.

WHEN, HOW, and WHO you ask, if thought out and practiced with intention, will help give you a clearer sense of the individual situation and provide a broader overview. Which in turn will take away more of the sense of entitlement to help better articulate your wants and needs. In life, we will always be asking for something, but better to do so with humility, especially when it's a challenging situation.

Be a good person because you should. Not because you're expecting something in return.

Living in a manner that you know to be righteous and true can be a constant struggle. It takes patience, understanding, compassion and, at times, forgiveness. There are periods when "living right" seems to offer little or no return. If fact, you may even watch others who cut corners, or don't have any regard for anyone but themselves, "get ahead". But don't be fooled. Life is a marathon and the beauty of it is that it will continue to repeat the same lessons until you learn them. Being a kind person and taking care of others should be all the reward you seek. The moment you have expectations from these actions is the moment they become null and void. Bringing us full circle into the premise of this chapter, in that the world owes you nothing, even if you do the right things.

Being a good person and doing the right things applies to everyone, rich or poor, black, or white, man or women. It is my opinion that if you are lucky enough to have financial success, you have even more responsibility to maintain a humble and grateful demeanor. I see many people who have great resources and the ability to help others, but they don't. Although it's true that it should not be expected, even receiving a smile or some kind and encouraging words shouldn't be difficult. Sadly, it can be, which portrays the disposition of "being better than" or "too good for".

On the flip side of this coin, if you have a hard and challenging life, or you are down on your luck, the worst thing you can do is become bitter and feel as though you're a victim. When we are low, it's easy to stay there and feel sorry for ourselves while lashing out at others. In times of hardship, the last thing we feel like doing is being nice to others, but the sooner we show some kindness and get up and push forward, the more likely it is that our luck will change. Rich or poor, we all have situations that can tempt us to fall into an entitled frame of mind and in either case, it doesn't do us any good. If we have money, no one owes us more respect, but we owe everyone mutual respect. If we are poor, no one owes us any help, but we owe it to ourselves to keep getting up and pushing through. To find nobility in one's suffering is the fastest way to learn from the situation.

When nothing good or proactive can be done or said, it's a good idea to walk away. I have been in many situations where my anger and lack of understanding gave me nothing good to say in those moments. I learned the "48 hour rule", which is when you give anything that pushed your buttons or left you heated, 48 hours, most of the time you will either be over it, or in a much better place to see the situation more clearly. It doesn't mean that you were wrong to be upset, but it can save you and the other people involved a much worse outcome than when you react rashly.

Find peace in yourself.

This is one of the most important topics in this book and truly one of the few remedies for understanding that the world doesn't owe you anything. It is also one of life's biggest struggles and will be an ongoing battle for the rest of our lives. There is not "one way" to find peace in yourself. I don't know all the answers and would never attempt to overstep my scope. I can say that in my experience, just knowing that the more peace we find within, if we choose to look there, the less we are affected by people's thoughts or opinions and the less we feel we are owed. Letting go of expectations of others in this way empowers you to look within, for only you can truly know the depths of what work you need to do.

Thinking you are owed something is only a distraction that delays the bigger and deeper questions. Have you ever taken the time to think about what you owe yourself? To me, this question has much more meaning and potential when we stop expecting anything from anyone and start putting the entire responsibility on ourselves. Our sole focus can then be on our own desires, abilities, or shortcomings. Which, when worked on, empowers us beyond the limiting thought that we are owed anything. We can often find peace through our vocation, faith, family, health and numerous other things in life.

The point is when we move away from "what is owed to us", we release that baggage, which opens a path for productivity and enhancement. As we strive for this mindset, it becomes more easily accepted that we are truly owed nothing and our life is dictated by our thoughts and actions.

This is the ultimate freedom and what I believe we should strive for, as we are no longer enslaved by wants or needs, but liberated by the peace of mind we have cultivated within.

CHAPTER 9

FULFILLMENT LIES IN ACCOMPLISHMENT
(Except, the perfect action has no result)

> *"There is no path to peace, peace is the path."*
> —GANDHI

As we continue on this path, there are times when I pause and reflect. When coming up with the chapter titles, it was never my intention to have them rooted in a juxtaposition type format. But the more I thought about it, the more I realized that life in this context makes sense. Living becomes more a game of balance if we are in tune with truth. This, of course, is much easier said than done when it's hard enough just to make ends meet, never mind also trying to inspire one's own fulfillment.

Truth be told, much of the journey is often missed because of how focused we are on accomplishment, failing to realize that 95 percent of the work is what leads us to the goal. Then we often take no time to savor what we achieve and start back on the empty cycle of "the next thing". For many, the "great accomplishment" leaves people with a hollow sense of yearning and questions about why their thirst for deep fulfillment has not been quenched. Like good worker ants, we jump back in the fringe and hope that this time around we will be struck by a revelation that "explains it all" or exposes "the meaning of life". Sadly, this rarely happens…

The truth about fulfillment is embodied in plain sight. Each moment of the process is the only thing that matters. The byproduct is the result, and the end is rarely what we expect. Just because we work for something doesn't guarantee our success, which is another reason why finding one's fulfillment in the process should become the priority.

We all have dreams and goals that will not come to fruition, and many invest days, months, years, or even a lifetime of commitment. Far too often, the fantasy of the accomplishment blinds people and drives them to a place of obsession and ruthless ambition, where they justify their actions for the "sake of the goal". From my personal experience, I can attest to being gripped by this mind frame, only to "wake up" years later with more questions than answers. Being driven is a remarkable attribute, which few people truly embody consistently. It is in these minds that great achievements are born and can be said, have changed the world. It is also why it is hard to blame someone on this path, especially when they trip and fall on their way to the top. As a society, we often declare these "mishaps" justifications for the "ultimate accomplishment" and part of the path toward what we truly want. However, how many times do people reflect with regret, remorse, shock, or resentment, and realize later that "hindsight is twenty-twenty"?

I don't know about you, but I'm tired of hearing the same old narrative. Being a person who fell into the tight clenches of "fulfillment and accomplishments" as my main focus, I feel some insight is needed for others, specifically in a way that helps prevent collateral damage from being so lost in one's accomplishments. Some say it's the human condition and we must learn on our own, but I think having more perspective before you embark on your quest, can provide relief when you need it most, versus running blind into what has led many people to a dismal place.

What is balance? Is it possible?

This is a loaded question and means many different things to different people. Yet, having a better grasp on what balance means for you is an important step in reducing the dramatic counterbalance that life presents.

The ultra-marathon runner and fitness enthusiast David Goggins may consider the idea that you can't run twenty miles a day or do 100 pull ups, a weak mindset. For Mr. Goggins, his "proof" is measured in miles and being able to constantly push his physical boundaries, where others may find his approach obsessive and unnatural. Neither is incorrect, and the only "right" way for each person lies within.

From this standpoint, you can see that balance can only truly be found and defined by the individual. The "accomplishment" has no distinct meaning except for the person. It can then be better understood that each result may become inconsequential for anyone besides the singular mind that determined it. There is no baseline, average, or normalcy. The purest determining factor becomes knowing if you gave it everything you had in any situation. Leaving behind no regret, and no stone unturned. You must drop all comparison to measure the truth about what balance means for you. Each of our lives is unique and builds us with certain needs, wants, likes, dislikes, which, in turn, propels us to find our "balance". Frankly, many people may never feel the need to run five miles straight in their lifetime, let alone twenty miles a day. But that is okay. The point just proves that there are different paths for each of us and different forms of what we deem balanced.

A perfect action has no results.

You are likely asking what does this mean and how does it tie into balance? In my observations, we are at our best in life when we find our center, when what we do becomes an extension of our deeper self and becomes all-encompassing. Understanding at this level takes deep commitment, discipline, resilience, and patience and often is riddled with setbacks along the way. It is like a moving target that you have to eventually accept versus trying to change or control. It is also good to note that although it may look "easy" or "effortless" in moments when we hit our deepest sense of flow, it takes a great deal of energy to produce. But in those moments that manifest, when everything comes together, there is nothing more to seek. No higher place, no worry or regret; just the extension of one instance to the next, creating a sense of flow. Some call it perfection, others consider it the byproduct of being in "the zone". But I like to think if it as what we have already put in motion, becoming what it is meant to be. Not an accomplishment, not fulfillment, but the truest form of the moment. These "actions" are constantly happening and whether we see them or not (often we don't) has no bearing on the outcomes. Thus, the perfect action can have no result. It is just another disbursement of energy that continues in its destined path, already gone before we can define it, already moving onward.

Make decisions based on the moment, not on what you want to avoid.

The basis of this section is a continuation of what we covered earlier in this chapter regarding specifically failing to realize that the path (or 95 percent of the work), is what actually leads us to the goal. But if you take another step back and have a good look before you head down any path, you may be surprised by what inspires your motivation. Brace yourself. Are you ready?

Often the objects of or desires (people and relationships included) are only a reaction to not wanting to feel what is going on in the moment.

Let that soak in and be honest with yourself. More importantly, be clear and mindful of your emotions and thought process from start to finish, specifically when you are honed in on something you desire. Often, wanting or expecting something is a reaction, not a thoughtful process that determines the root of where the yearning stems from.

A good example is after the end of a painful relationship or the passing of a loved one. Both can create a great deal of grief and agony and most people try to avoid the pain at all costs, repeatedly and automatically, which is when the default response of desire kicks in. Instead of facing the pain, we run and distract ourselves, avoiding hard conversations that require us to deal with the issues. Examples include:

- Blaming the other person and not taking any accountability

- Being forgetful
- Joking, laughing, or being cold in inappropriate situations
- Alcohol or drugs
- Jumping into another relationship
- Working constantly
- Becoming extremely isolated

While some responses are innate and instilled to protect us from the overload of traumatic experiences, there will always come a time when you cannot run away, and life will force you to look at the cause of the pain. The sooner we accept and understand this, the quicker we can embrace the pain, which in turn speeds up our healing process. If you incorporate this insight, it can also make future situations more palatable and future relationships healthier. A sign of a loving and healthy relationship is not only how you deal with good times, but also being able to know how to argue and disagree. If one party fails to engage or lacks a "map" to help them navigate uncomfortable conversations, the desire to avoid and feel something else then ensues.

You cannot feel all the good and not the bad; life doesn't work that way. So next time you face a difficult situation, watch what your default reaction is. If not redirected, the difference between the reality of what is, versus the desire to not want to feel that truth, can keep you running for the rest of your life.

No accomplishments? No desire? Now what?

The point of this book, is to help you think and grow. I can say that I have turned these views and perceptions over and over and at times I still come up empty or confused. But I have also accepted what I feel are the deeper fundamentals, which help us improve and realize the peace within, that is always present, but often forgotten.

I continually implement the fundamentals covered in this book, and have seen that my life no longer operates on reactions, but from a calmer place of clarity and understanding. This does not mean that clarity or understanding always comes easily, but I've found that living through the lens of truth is far more fulfilling than living a life built in the fog of misguided desire and blind accomplishments. The statement "ignorance is bliss" in this situation has never rung truer for me, and I believe is what we all should continuously push to move beyond.

When the seeds of accomplishment manifest through the process, rather than as a knee-jerk reaction or self-indulgence, we start to see the difference in the quality of our lives. No longer led by fear, but guided by our own truth, we experience each moment as the only fulfillment we need, instead of it always being at the end of an accomplishment.

CHAPTER 10

YOU CAN ONLY DIE ONCE
(Except when you understand you really must die each day)

> *"The Tragedy of life is not death,*
> *but what we let die inside of us while we live."*
> —UNKNOWN

The afflictions that life often delivers tend to leave wounds. When I heard "Time gives us the ability to live with our scars", I thought that was more appropriate for real life than a Disney movie. When you accept that all of us have scars, some very deep and life altering, you begin to realize that individuals that have embraced them, regardless, may be on to something. Their attitudes are a key factor in how they view life and the way they navigate the hard times.

My uncle fought in World War II in the first infantry, and I was told stories by my family of the horrors he saw. Not once would he discuss this with us, but you could see a look in his eyes. A depth of intensity, mixed with pain, love, fear and hate, that only people who have been in those kinds of situations show. Yet, Uncle Ernie was the softest spoken, most kind and funny man you could ever meet. He loved his family and would touch my nephews' and nieces' faces, with the most gentle caress you could imagine. His hands looked like worn leather that had been forged into steel. He would smile and laugh and say, "God Hito, isn't this the most beautiful thing you have ever seen"? To me, that is what it means to let go, or "die" in that moment and only be concerned with what is, not what was.

If anyone had a reason to be bitter, resentful or "dead inside" it was this man. War forever changes a person. This is a fact, but how it changes you is your choice. Even towards the end of his life, my uncle accepted his fate and took it with no sense of resentment. He was a heavy smoker (loved his Marlboros) and was diagnosed with stage four lung cancer while approaching his 80s. When we spoke with him, there seemed to be no fear, just a quiet peace and acceptance of life and no change in his kind and loving disposition. Through it all, and until his death, he continued to smoke as much as he did during his entire life. He said, "I got this far going this way, no reason to change it up now"! My uncle's life taught me a lot, the constant example of how well he composed himself, even after all he had gone through. I would always think that if he could be so patient and kind, I had no excuse. It has never left me, and I often reference our time together when my life seems to be fighting its own wars. I can think back and see the truth in his eyes, with a Marlboro hanging off his lip, cool and calm, a voice that sounded like a mix of Clint Eastwood and Frank Sinatra saying, "Everything is okay, Hito, it's just life" as he laughed and took a deep drag.

My uncle tried to make me understand that the only easy day was yesterday, but as a young boy with an obvious lack of life experience, I missed the completeness in what he was insinuating with his cigarette smoke lingering, haiku style responses. Leaving me with many holes to fill as life progressed and with many mistakes along the way. A theoretical understanding of life only holds so much weight, and it is not until we get knee deep in it we find out how prepared we are. In many cases, we are not equipped, and the consequences lead us to contaminated mind frames, that although may keep us alive, or "protected" in the moment, serve us poorly in the long run. This is even more reason to let it die. I'll expand:

To acknowledge that you may be reactive and defaulting back to these habits is an important step. But how do you know? Especially if you have been doing it most of your life. A good way is to be aware of your body and listen to your heart. I like the term "Spidey Sense" and it is usually very effective in situations if you are coming from an honest, clear place.

Does the response feel natural or forced?
If it feels forced, then that is a sign that you're more worried about what you want to get from the situation, or protecting yourself, than anything else, which is not a healthy sign of balance, nor does it show respect for other people.

Does it make you, or the other person uncomfortable?
Although we cannot be responsible for how others feel, there is a level of awareness and reflection that is required in all forms of how we act and what we say and when we say it. If you see the same uncomfortable reactions and patterns with other people, it's a high likelihood you're the common denominator, not the world. Of course, if you don't feel

comfortable yourself, but still proceed, maybe your current mindset overrides your sense of reason. Again, another warning that something needs to change.

Is the response more of an automatic reaction, or is it something you have to think about deeply beforehand? Minds engrained with these attitudes are locked and loaded and ready to fire before they even know the whole situation. It's like verbal diarrhea. Reaction-based mindsets can be very destructive and lack empathy or reason. Typically, if you have removed these defaults, your desire to have everyone win trumps your desire to be right.

Are you able to think about the other person at all, or does the focal point have to revolve around you? The stories of our past, if not released, can define how we see and react to everything. If we have been abused, then everyone can become an abuser. If we have been abandoned, then everyone will someday leave, and the list goes on. It's so often that the things we shun or resent about our past are the same things we have become. Once this dominates, you can become very egocentric and correlate everything with relation to yourself. This manifests those stories into reality because of the lack of ability to assess the current moment, with the appropriate mindset or lens. Another indicator that you must let this die if you are to truly live.

HOW TO DIE

All of us hold on to what we think represents us. In our mind, without having a specific identity or persona, then we feel we may fade into the great abyss of life, never to be heard, seen, understood, or loved, or not able to defend ourselves. But what we fail to recognize is that the same unique and "independent" "character" we take on and instill, the more we push what we truly want away. We create self-imposed requirements and expectations that divide us based on these made-up fronts, instead of being free to extend our true nature. The lens that may have once served you well and enabled your survival is now the thing that is stopping your growth. The "biker chick", only wears black, has a "dark heart" and is a proclaimed introvert, with piercings and tattoos, meets the "businessman", who dresses in suits, is outgoing and drives sports cars. Looking at it from our "identities" it's hard to see a match. But strip away the self-imposed ideals, and the possibilities for deeper connections soon appear, revealing their hearts are closer than we think. The "biker chick" might love animals and enjoy cooking or folding laundry, while the "businessman" may also be introverted, and recently started playing the guitar. A genuine opportunity to connect may never manifest, all because we cannot let go of our fears and facades that have become such a part of our nature we have forgotten our true self and what we really desire.

But to get there, to remember our true hearts and our innocence and vulnerabilities, requires stepping onto a ledge and until we let our old self die, there will always be a barrier. Our views will never be clear, for we will always look at each moment through a lens from the past. But most people would rather live in this fog, instead of facing the pain. They would rather live with the discomfort and limp along. Sadly, this is what most of us do and justify it by the persona we build and enable.

To die each day means to let go of the past, while not trying to find ways and means to avoid it. Pain and despair can never be dissolved through escape. Only by being aware can you feel what love is not, then you may come to understand what love and truth are. You cannot tell death to wait for you until you are ready. When we actually die, everything in motion ends without argument. Your job, your role in the family, everything you have not done, stops, there is no more time. This is why it is so crucial to find out how to live your life now, today, in which there is always a conclusion to everything you start. Not in your workplace, but inside yourself. To end all your hurts, painful memories, and the comparing to others. To pursue the end of these things each day is to let them die. Which will then allow your mind and heart to be fresh, clear, and young. If you are willing and able to comply, a mind like this can never be wounded and brings us back to our innocence and true self.

As you start to live this way, the pain of the old life often clings to you. The depth of the fear and guilt inside can become so overpowering that at times it seems unbearable. But holding steadfast to the moment, the quality of your mind and life becomes timeless. You understand what it means to die each day without fear, and the peace and freedom that follows becomes your reality. You learn that love is a part of this path because love is always new, always eternal, always in truth.

The deeper we go, the more we come to realize how busy our lives are, but more importantly, how busy our minds are. In society, we tend to let our outside world dictate things, but in truth, it's our inside world that creates our reality. This is not to say that our lives are not filled with work, family, friends and everything that encompasses the human condition. But taking the approach of harnessing your peace within provides our day-to-day life with the balance and assistance that we fail to establish without clear intention.

STEP 1—*Step away from your phone. It will be okay.*
In today's world, the name of the game is speed and instant gratification. With social media updates each second and the intentional hook that all of our technology platforms facilitate, combined with the daily demands of life, it is rare we come up for air. Our minds are constantly bombarded and the consequences are steadily being revealed. "Faster" is typically thought to be better, but when things go so fast you can't fundamentally absorb them, problems ensue. I'm not the extremist that will tell you technology is bad and that we must completely disconnect. The fact is whether we like it or not, the future is now, and technology is a major part of that. The obvious pros are many and should be used for their intended purposes, which can be to help streamline, simplify, better organize, and to stay connected to family and friends wherever they may be. But this is not what is happening, and our minds and hearts are being adversely affected. To find clarity, you need to be still sometimes. Step away from the phone. It will be okay.

STEP 2—*Take a chance and connect with real people*
Humans need to congregate and require a genuine connection. As referenced in the previous step regarding technology, we are making it harder to unplug and easier to stay stuck in digital worlds. As ridiculous as it sounds, we seem to have forgotten that interactions with other humans keep us on our toes and hone our communication and social

skills. Each person you meet in real life will have a different opinion, interpretation, and story, which will require us to react accordingly and sometimes make us confused or uncomfortable. This explains why some people stay in their digital worlds. They think they can control the environment. For a short term plan, this may work, but in the long term it has dire consequences and is seen in the increase in anxiety and declining social abilities in our society. Personally, I see it everywhere, and it saddens me. I always try to be kind and will ask how someone's day is going when I meet them at the grocery store. I often get glares of surprise or bewilderment, or even worse. On occasion, I have gotten frowns or other responses that show they are uncomfortable with social interaction. Wow! This is a byproduct of not having real connections with live humans. Connections with others give us much needed perspective and pull us out of our own little worlds, bringing us closer and providing the feeling of unity we crave. Take a chance and connect with people.

STEP 3—*Find nature*
There is nothing like feeling a cool breeze while walking in a forest, hearing a river flow, a bird singing, or dipping your toes into the ocean. In these moments, you experience the beauty of what's in front of you, and ironically, it is this simplistic stillness that can create peace within. The peace and energy you get when you step out of hustle and bustle and into nature is undeniable and should be part of our regular maintenance and well-being. In the past, it was very difficult for me to take time off or get away into nature. Habitually, I would justify my desire not to fall behind or lose momentum at work. It wasn't until almost being burnt out that I allowed myself to be coerced into it. But

once I settled into nature, I would feel the shift mentally, emotionally and spiritually and on each occasion when I returned to regular life, I would be more grounded and calm, which would lead to better creativity and production. Now I take getaways much more frequently as even a walk in the park can give a much-needed boost. The more we embrace nature and incorporate it into our lives, the better we operate. It's that simple. Find nature.

STEP 4—*Get rid of set conditions and order*
Nothing in life ever remains constant, thus why should you? The moment you plan your life according to a pattern, you are no longer living freely. Standing firmly to "what should be" puts you right back into your imagined persona. To be free of the past, you must see order in the moment, not in the future. Freedom is now. When talking about order, I mean regarding relationships and the now. When we think of planning, obviously we must prepare at a certain level. Building a business or flying to mars, needs a design.

Goodness in one's heart is the only true sense of order and following that in each situation, before defaulting back to set conditions, will always result in the most fluid outcome. To approach life in this manner, you must have strength and conviction. Often the right thing for us to do does not lead to what we expect. It can even leave us feeling misunderstood or even shortchanged in certain moments. Nonetheless, the resistance to delay gratification now for the future begins to turn into a way of life. Examples of this are frequent. Let's say a customer at your job is not happy and provides some pretty harsh, but accurate feedback. Your boss is having a tough month and the timing couldn't be worse. The easy decision is to quietly sweep it under the rug and not cause any more friction, but the better action would be to face the situation. Of course, when, and how you face it is just as crucial, but ignoring it rarely leads to anything good. A great rule of thumb I once heard is "Always tell the truth or don't lie".

Another constant struggle with this can happen in our personal relationships. Let's say you and your significant other have been fighting a lot lately and things don't seem to be headed in the right direction or getting any better. You start to see that their past is preventing them (and you) from moving forward. But the subject is very painful and traumatic and any time this comes up, your partner does not want to deal with it. If you say they should not force the issue and will address it when "ready", this could become an extremely difficult situation for you. By all means encourage them to move at a pace they are comfortable with, but this begs the question: how long will it take? A month, year, five years? Are you supposed to guess, or just wait until that time comes? What if, for you, not dealing with these issues is causing major pain and conflict, which has already shown to have continual negative effects on your relationship? Many would just stay silent, risking other issues down the road.

A truthful statement from you could be, "I know this is a very painful situation and how much you are suffering, but I feel that the longer this goes unaddressed, the more it impacts our ability to fully connect. I don't want you to feel I'm trying to force you to deal with it on my time and know you can only make that decision when you are ready. That is why am asking for some kind of plan, so I have a better understanding of what that looks like and see if I'm able to give you all the love and support you need to get there. Otherwise, we are just stuck, and I will need to decide if we can continue forward." Of course, you can still be judged as selfish and insensitive. But if that is your truth and you are coming from a place of love, compassion and understanding, then you must follow it for your peace of mind, even it means a consequence or outcome you don't desire.

The same goes for your partner. If they are not ready, willing, or able, to confront their past and if that means sacrificing the relationship because of it, that is a choice. And if that is their truth, then they must state it. Using "until I'm ready" as a position, is controlling and manipulative and gives no accountability for decisions or actions. A truthful statement would be "At this point I'm not sure how long it will take me to address these issues and heal, I know it's affecting our relationship and not giving you any idea of when I will be ready is not fair for either of us. I know you want something more concrete, but I'm just not there. If me not giving you an answer, means we cannot be together, I accept that". Or alternatively and just as true, "I'm not ready yet and instead of making you wait; I think it's best that we part ways". Of course, the optimistic option would be both people wanting each other more than their own desires or past traumas and setting a plan and battling through the ups and downs, as all relationships demand. But only when both people want to work for it can that happen. One person, no matter how strong, can steer this type of situation alone. If someone has their mind steadfast and with no desire to face the issues, then things won't move. Being stagnant can be just as bad as moving backwards, life is always moving and changing and for our well-being we must embrace it or face much suffering. Get rid of set conditions and order.

STEP 5—*Don't get too comfortable*
Humans have an uncanny ability to adapt and persevere. It is a dynamic

quality and is one of the obvious reasons we are at the top of the food chain. But if that is one of our superpowers, our kryptonite is getting too comfortable. As we all progress through life, it is imperative that we understand nothing is permanent, and change is inevitable. The most painful lessons are those that we fail to acknowledge and "never expect". But if we are honest with ourselves, there should be nothing that catches us off guard. At the forefront of our existence, relationships are again another example of this. To accept that all relationships will end with death clearly shows that they are temporary. Now ideally (maybe) we envision an extended period of time or "forever" as the baseline. A classic portrayal is a couple marries and lives out their days until old age and death. Though in some cases this does occur, for a vast majority, the end comes much sooner.

Personally, I was in the mindset that the time in a relationship equated the depth, connection, and love it delivered. While it can be true in many facets that more time deepens and strengthens certain attributes, it wasn't until after I experience both a long and a short relationship, and both provided equal depth and impact, that I changed my mind.

I think that the narrative of "more time in a relationship is better" needs to be analyzed. We all know couples who have been together "forever" but who don't appear to be happy at all. Who over the years have gotten comfortable in a manner that promotes a toxic cycle of collusion, guilt, and control, versus a truthful ability to coexist. A crude saying I once heard that stuck with me was, "If you live in shit long enough, you begin to get used to how it smells". Many people focus more on quantity than quality. This is a prime example of getting too comfortable, even when you are miserable. This behavior also echoes through work, family, friends, health and many other habits of "comfort" that leave us more disabled then empowered.

Turning our attention to short relationships, there can be a great deal of abundance within them. People may come into our lives at the perfect time, only in our minds, to depart too soon. Nonetheless, the lessons can be numerous if a connection was made and can propel you to a better understanding of yourself. Of course, serial relationships can be just another means of comfort, knowing inside from the start that there's no authentic connection, often promotes a cheap thrill (if you're lucky) and leaves both people no better off than where they started.

As you can see, comfort can lie in any spectrum of any experience. Extremes on both fronts are always lurking and may justify their frameworks, which just end up enabling another kind of comfort. With all this said, there is nothing wrong with enjoying the comforts of life. In fact, without them, our existence would be bleak and provide little meaning. The trick is enjoying them as they enter our lives, whether they for fifty years or four months, making sure you are fully maximizing each instance for the sake of the beauty in what it provides, not in its length of time. Growing means change, and change is not easy, but is always where we gain the most insight. Don't get too comfortable.

HOW TO LIVE

With all this talk about letting things die, I hope I have revealed how it ties into how to live. Many of the concepts in this book are not new, yet we often float along in life without a course or become stuck to ideals that have long ceased to serve us in their intended purpose. When our maps run out, instead of it being a bad thing, we can take it as an opportunity to grow and move beyond stagnant mind frames.

Being unfamiliar with anything often means starting over, which means being a novice, which means having humility, but it will also broaden your range and quality of life. If you haven't noticed yet, life will continue to give you the same lessons until you are ready to learn them, so the sooner you hone in on that concept, the better chance you will have to blossom into your truest form. Everyone has limitless potential, but without clear intention and action, then we will rarely see it manifest. If we maintain the status quo and hope that what we want falls into our lap, we end up waiting our whole life, when all it may have taken was a first step towards what we feared.

Making fear your friend is another good item to have on the agenda, because 99% of the time when you face it, it's not as scary or overwhelming as you imagined. If we stop changing or moving because of fear, we succumb to a life only half lived.

> *"Life is short, break the rules. Forgive quickly, kiss slowly.*
> *Love truly. Laugh uncontrollably*
> *and never regret anything that makes you smile."*
> —MARK TWAIN

CHAPTER 11

A LETTER. DEAR TREVOR. IT IZ WHAT IT IZ *(Conclusion)*

Dear Trevor,

Much time has passed since I last saw you. I'm happy to report that life has settled, and I have found my way back to some kind of normalcy. I left my old job and was able to break away from that God forsaken industry. At times I miss it, but never enough to regret leaving, but just enough to smile sometimes. Like when you used to bring me lunch unexpectedly, or when you would message me things that would make me LOL and have other employees stare at me in confusion after my outburst. But when it was time to go, I did. In fact, I ran so fast out of there I thought at the same time I could outrun you; I could outrun us. For a while it worked, being caught up in the "new" gives little room for feelings. It's a great device in tough situations (highly recommend it/ smirking), but like anything in life, it will wear off eventually. So as the new car smell faded, I made another left-brain decision and went back to school. I'll never forget the story you told me about your choice to go back to school and how much you tried to show me I could too. The whole time I thought I could never get there, but the whole time you knew I could. Covertly. (Not really, you could always see me. Dammit, I hated that. ;)) I was somewhat peeved by your "lack of understanding" of "just how hard" it would be for me to ever go back to school. Now that I think about it, it was more how much of my strength I couldn't see, but that you clearly did. I'm still back and forth about my major and as much as you wanted me to "follow my heart" and go to a drama or art school, I'm not sure I'm there yet. But hey, crazier things have happened, that is for sure.

As much as I want to forget about you, forget about us, as much as I want to jump on my bike and keep riding to the end of the world, I always do so with the thought of you. I want to tell myself I don't know why, but I do. I want to tell myself you were the right person at the wrong time and that is probably true. So many things that have settled, yet so many things unsettled.

When we met it was almost an instant connection and a fondness that I continually questioned, because I never knew something like this. I never could truly say what I felt or what I wanted, because I was scared it was only me, but in perfect harmony, you would say what I was thinking and feeling and how you shared it as well. How could this be? What was the catch? Yet you would rise again, hold me again, kiss me again and never waiver. It became clear that it was much more than a fling. It amazed me when you would send me songs that I was literally about to send you or laugh at things I thought only my crude sense of humor would enjoy. Oh, and laugh we did. So much fun, so much freedom. For a time, I was safe, I could rest with you in a way that I never could before. You literally gave me a weighted blanket and a heating pad to keep me okay when I was away from you, and showed me what the right pair of shoes could do. So much thought in each action and it did allow me to breathe, for a time. Now that I think

CHAPTER 11—A LETTER. DEAR TREVOR. IT IZ WHAT IT IZ. | 149

about it, I may have been making up for the rest that I could never find growing up.

Your touch was as deep as your smile, and when we kissed, I melted, and when we loved, every part of me was yours. We flowed in harmony and in those moments, I was able to understand my (Grinch heart) and your love. Our adventures were magnificent. You showed me things that I still think about, so much to recall, so much. Boats, planes, beaches, steam rooms and buffalo milk! After my first real massage, I came back to our room before you, and after my shower, while getting ready, I started to sing. You quietly came in and sat on the bed for a while and listened. When I did realize you were there, I asked how long you had been listening. With those deep peaceful and loving eyes, you told me, "Not long enough" and gently smiled and kissed my head. And that's only a slight mention of what was packed into our 4 months! So fast. Too fast?

When I found out the news, I didn't know what to do. I was scared beyond belief, and it was almost impossible to see or feel anything else. Tunnel vision ensued. Where most men would have run away or become distant, you came on stronger and did all you could to comfort me. 4 months! So much fear, so much confusion, so much embarrassment. The "what if's" ran amuck, and all I wanted was to start over. When I told you, that I almost wasn't going to tell you the news, you looked at me as if you were lost. Old habits die hard, I suppose, and I panicked. 4 months! When you asked me to be yours, I wanted nothing more than to say yes. I wanted it all. But I was too scared and did not think making that kind of decision based on the circumstances was smart. Or at least that's what I was telling myself. You were always so loving, so kind, and even through my fits, you would stay with me. I know when I told you no, you were hurt, your pride was bruised. But know it wasn't because I didn't want to say yes. I always wanted to say yes.

After the loss, I was relieved and scared at the same time. I know you were at peace with everything because I knew we both did not expect this and would let God and life take its course. You were even ready to keep moving on together. But I wasn't. And then I ran. You told me that you wanted all of me. But inside I was still so impacted by the real possibility of what we had just been through, I didn't think I could fully open back up to you in all ways, for a long while. I know how much loving me meant to you, especially the physical relationship, and I just didn't think I could give you what you needed. So Fast! I could not imagine being able to replicate what we had experienced and that the stars had aligned for that short time and that instead of chancing it, I should get out while I was ahead. I knew completely who you were and what our love could be, but I wanted to get out of your way. I'm not asking you to understand. I'm not sure if you ever could. I'm not even sure why I wrote this, except you are in my dreams. I can't say much more, all I can say is, It iz what it iz.

Always, Your Sweetie ♥
PS I love you

I decided to conclude this book with a "letter to Trevor" that embodies all the possibilities of a love that was not able to lift off. Again, we all hope for happily ever after, but after we experience life for an extended period, love and relationships tend to surprise us. Our maps run out. You would think that we would learn, or at least be somewhat prepared for pitfalls and curveballs, but when love gets a hold of us, tunnel vision ensues. It can be a good thing, but it can also blind us to the realities we don't want to see.

The tie in with everything we've covered is that nothing can, nor should be assumed. New maps need to be made constantly, new "upgrades", and we must leave no stone unturned.

Reading this, I guess you did not see this coming and perhaps expected a more traditional conclusion. But that is also the point and the beauty of life. Sometimes we catch lightning in a bottle when we least expect. The trick is to be grateful for the time and experience. The reality is that life is always changing. What was once a beautiful union, a dance that opened your heart, can turn in a different direction. And once it does, the next trick is to accept the moment, not base it on the past and lose hope for the future. Much easier said than done. When your mind is like a prison, whose only way to freedom is to let go, then for your sake, you must. You must also forgive, show compassion and be grateful, doing all you can to extract the beauty of what was, to free the reality of what is.

This "letter" was about how two souls were each given tremendous gifts and lived more in a few months, then most do in a lifetime. No one said life wouldn't be messy, but that's the beauty of it and a wise person once said. It iz what it iz…

www.ingramcontent.com/pod-product-compliance
Lightning Source LLC
Chambersburg PA
CBHW071244070526
44583CB00017B/2319